PETERS' PRINCIPLES OF SUCCESS

COMMON SENSE PATHWAYS TO PROSPERITY AND FULFILLMENT

LENNY PETERS, M.D.

Published in the United States by Lenny Peters Foundation
645 North Main Street
High Point, NC 27262
(336) 901-0029
lennypetersfoundation.org

All author proceeds from the sale of this book will be donated to help orphans and terminally ill people worldwide through the Lenny Peters Foundation. For more information, please contact lennypetersfoundation@gmail.com.

ISBN (hardcover) 979-8-218-04983-6
ISBN (eBook) 979-8-218-04984-3

Library of Congress Control Number: 2022915394

Cover design by Laura Duffy
Book design by Yvonne Parks at PearCreative.ca

Printed in the United States of America

CONTENTS

FOREWORD

There is a genuine skill to being in the right place at the right time. We have each probably missed this proverbial *sweet spot* at more crossroads in our lives than we might have wished. A few times, however, I have been lucky. Or smart. At least, smart enough to recognize my luck. In any case, I do not believe anyone would confuse my passel of moments of good fortune with my possessing any such skill.

On one such occasion, I was both lucky and smart enough to recognize that a man I had written somewhat frequently about as a journalist for a local business publication had taken a shine to me. He liked my writing and saw potential in some other skills I might have unknowingly demonstrated in some of our few but lengthy interactions.

When I finally summoned the courage and struck out on my own as a freelancer, just about the same time Covid was reaching its first peak in the United States, this man became one of my earliest and most loyal clients. As the pandemic wore on and other clients began to feel the pinch, I had fewer and fewer jobs thrown my way, save for one—Dr. Lenny Peters. I soon realized he was not necessarily coming to me with work because he needed it. He was doing so because he knew I needed it, and he was well-positioned to provide it.

Dr. Peters' patronage slowly morphed into a sort of mentorship. And when he decided he needed to take a step back from some of the day-to-day operations he was accustomed to overseeing and was nearing the completion of the hand-off of the bulk of his business interests to his daughter as part of their longstanding and patiently executed succession plan, he brought me into the fold full-time.

It is from this perspective that, for readers who will not have the benefit of knowing him or knowing him closely, I hope to introduce the man whose insights you will receive in this book, some or all of which might do more than inform but also inspire the rest of your very personal quest toward your unique vision of success. For success has as many faces as the number of people living in the world today. It means something different to each of us. And determining what it means to you as early as you can in your journey will help accelerate your path toward the realization of whatever that vision is.

This requires a level of readiness, maturity, and a willingness to let go of contrived notions and naivete. It means being open-minded. It means knowing who you are and what you want from life and from yourself. You may not have all these answers right now, and that is OK. Knowing that this should be your starting point will better prepare you to receive the messages contained within this book and—I am willing to bet, if you are truly committed to achieving the success you envision for yourself—are already coming to you from other corners of the universe.

Dr. Lenny Peters, born in Kerala, India, in a village with a name filled with consonants I can never seem to remember the order of, managed to rise from a shoeless existence as a boy to overseeing a small empire of a business portfolio bearing his name. He did so by learning the skill of being in the right place at the right time. That is not to say he knew when to show up to receive anything being doled out freely, no. It means he did what it took to ready himself to be able to see and to seize the very opportunity he had been envisioning and preparing for, however many years in advance.

In life, as in business, those who seem to always be in the right place at the right time have more truthfully manifested their success through hard work, sound decisions, discipline, and a fine-tuned instinct developed over time. In a sports context, everyone sees the winning shot to beat the buzzer, but no one sees the thousands of free throws and three-point shots thrown up in a darkened gym day after day. Off-season workouts, post-game shooting marathons, and meticulous attention paid to the fundamentals are what build champions.

This is less a book about achieving success than it is about preparing for it. And I can think of no one better equipped to share his experience in doing so over the span of a lifetime. In his first foray into authorship, Dr. Peters recounted in detail his journey from a penniless, shoeless boyhood in the rice patties of India to overseeing the rise of a multifaceted portfolio of interests which includes the largest independent health care provider in the state of North Carolina, commercial real estate holdings and development, banking, medical research, and clinical trials.

As he acknowledges in his autobiographical debut, *Barefoot to Benefactor: My Life Story of Faith and Courage*, at any point along the journey, Dr. Peters could have cashed in his chips and lived out the rest of his days in luxury anywhere in the world. Sure, he has his nests to which he escapes in Manhattan and Miami, and perhaps in other parts of the world he does not disclose even to a close friend such as me. Yet he refuses to walk away from what he describes as his calling, to heal and help others.

If I knew nothing else about the man, that alone would inspire my respect. However, when he asked me to write this foreword for his new book sharing his insights on the main principles that have guided his success in life, I realized what makes him such a unique figure—one aptly suited to truly educate others in pursuit of their own dreams.

He could have asked any of his big-wig counterparts, the CEOs and Market Presidents of this bank or that, this Fortune 500 Company or the other. He could have asked any of the numerous politicians and financiers with whom he has dined at White House dinners or between tennis and tea at a prestigious country club to which I might otherwise be denied entry if I weren't in his company.

The realization I came to is the same principle I learned from the best military leaders I encountered in my brief time in the U.S. Air Force and which the toughest editors I had the pleasure of working under instilled in me during my 10-year career in journalism. As the editor-in-chief of a 12-person newsroom running a six-day daily community newspaper, I sought to employ this principle, and it served me well. The key tenet is this: recognize the talent in the people around you and position them as best you can so they might grow and become successful. The unfit will weed themselves out, and the talented and the committed will grow beyond your expectations and their own if granted the trust and the resources to do so.

Nothing worth having is handed to us. We must work for it, earn it, and learn to sustain it. That requires education and training, certainly. It also requires an opportunity. So many far more skilled or ambitious writers than I will never have some of the opportunities I have encountered because of fate, circumstances, or because they were unable to recognize the opening when it presented itself to them.

Furthermore, no mission is as well-executed or project expertly completed as when the right team is assembled and empowered to carry out what is expected. Dr. Peters knows this perhaps better than anyone I have ever come across because, despite his God-given intellect and the faith instilled in him by his mother, he has only been able to achieve all he has accomplished because people he came across in life saw something in him and believed in him. Even strangers who had never met the man were touched by the way others spoke on his behalf, and so they opened their homes or granted him a necessary introduction to help usher him along his path.

So, while I am an award-winning journalist, a published author and poet, an artist, and a budding podcaster and public speaker, I am not someone whom I would have thought a prominent figure such as he would seek out to—hopefully—draw readers in at the outset of his second published work. Therein lies the magic of the man and why his words which will follow mine and fill the chapters of this book might very well serve you, the reader, regardless of where you might be in your own journey toward success. You might find yourself hiding in those chapters, displaying some of the very skills and habits included, or, better still, knowing you lack some habit or attribute and finding the strength to admit it and then do the work to acquire what is lacking.

For, if nothing else, it is the humility and humanity that eludes us which underpins our undoing. Yet when retained, or at worst rediscovered, these traits can redeem us and set us back on course. I trust it is his faith and his genuine desire to see his family and his community prosper rather than to suffer or struggle that drive the many goals and aspirations that keep a man who has accomplished so much from bowing out. And nowadays, in a post-Covid world where the challenges of the business landscape mirror those of daily life, where costs are higher and resources increasingly difficult to come by, we need leaders such as Dr. Peters. We need their knowledge and experience, their willingness to make tough decisions, and their innate ability to predict the future with a fair amount of accuracy. We need their mentorship so that the next generation and those that follow can learn to navigate a challenging world changing at a more rapid pace than ever before.

Technology and innovation have advanced far beyond offering modern conveniences; they now offer longer life, greater efficiency in energy creation and sustainability, and answers to medical and environmental issues that have long eluded science. Yet, while automation means some of the jobs and fields of previous generations will be erased, more jobs and new fields will be created to cope with and conquer a dawning era.

Leaders such as Dr. Peters are right now creating jobs, reshaping communities, and hiring and training the next generation of workers who will take over and build upon the legacies of those who came before. Investments and philanthropic support generated by the wealth and economic drivers put into motion by visionaries such as he will tomorrow pay untold dividends in positioning new leaders and innovators, thinkers, builders, teachers, doctors, and business leaders to carry us beyond the looming threats of rising sea levels, climate change, clean water and food scarcity, and increasingly deadly, difficult-to-contain outbreaks.

It may seem I've taken quite a leap here, but that is only because I have learned from Dr. Peters to not only look two steps ahead, but ten. And to examine not only the best possible outcome of any decision, but the worst as well. Somewhere in the middle, generally, lies the more realistic likelihood. And as he is fond of saying, an experienced, successful person might not have a crystal ball, but they can learn to be correct about 80 percent of the time when forecasting future trends, shifts, and outcomes.

In one more regard do we need more of Dr. Peters' ilk in the world—philanthropy. This is also one of the driving factors behind Dr. Peters forming his own charitable foundation, through which he and its board provide financial assistance and community support in his local area, as well as self-funding and operating 10 homes for orphan children, the sick, and the elderly in his native India and in South Africa. Those who are blessed to earn great sums of money also have a duty to give back, he often says.

I have learned from my own experiences and from close observation of Dr. Peters, of his daughter and President of the family companies, Elise Peters Carey, and of other successful men and women across myriad industries. What I have come to understand is that, while there is value in education and knowing all a textbook can impart, the ability to think critically, assess situations as they arise, identify skills and attributes in the people around you, and position and empower them to succeed are all components of what makes a great leader. That, and a willingness to be first no matter the risk if the outcome is determined to be worth the investment.

I challenge you to take this knowledge, along with the remaining insights and wisdom contained in this book and apply them to your own journey. And if you do not know and have a relationship with a person like Dr. Peters, perhaps in your city or within your field, find one. Introduce yourself and forge a relationship. That and the price of this book will be the best two investments you might ever make.

John Joyce
Global Director
The Lenny Peters Foundation
May 24, 2022

PREFACE

It is my hope, and my fervent belief, that the 10 principles herein—taken directly from my unorthodox and rather circuitous life journey—will inspire you with common-sense insights that illuminate your own path to prosperity and fulfillment.

But first: what *is* this thing we call "success"? Sure, prosperity is part of it. But it is more than simple monetary reward. Far more. For me, success connotes a fulfilling life, one in which we nurture our social, political, educational, and religious values.

In other words, I think of success as an *ideology*, rather than simply a financial yardstick, and I think if you've picked up this book and read this far, you agree with the assessment that success is less a destination and more a state of mind.

The reason there is no universal road map to success is because it is not a place that exists in the world, nor is it the solution to a quadratic equation or the result of a recipe for chocolate cake baked in your oven.

No, success is a continuous process. We maximize potential through effort and energy that, when consistently implemented over time, should increase one's productivity and capacity to achieve life goals at a rate which is suitable and sustainable over the course of one's life.

My recently published memoir makes it abundantly clear that, unlike many of you reading this book, I come from very humble beginnings as an immigrant from impoverished India. Through hard work, strong faith, and a commitment to treating people well and with dignity, I have climbed from a poor, literally shoeless existence in rural India to a position of wealth and status as an American.

My "success" is not a "one-size-fits-all" template. However, I do believe that the *principles* I set forth in this book hold universal benefits.

And I also believe that my principles are especially valuable in today's upside-down world, one in which our national economies are interlinked and ever-so-vulnerable, as fragile an enterprise as a string of mountaineers ascending K2, the second-highest peak in the Himalayas.

Businesses strive for success in the context of profits and losses, growth and expansion, outpacing the competition and winning market share. Sports teams measure success by wins and losses, championship rings, and league standings.

To my earlier point, we—as individuals—measure success in a variety of ways. Think in your mind of someone whom you might describe as successful. Criteria might include raising a family, owning a home, having or beginning to develop wealth, and possibly owning a business or being the CEO of a profitable company. In any of these examples one does not simply set a goal, meet it, and reap the rewards. No, there is always another goal, a bigger challenge, a setback, or an obstacle to overcome and a new reason to keep things moving forward. Like the above mountaineer metaphor, we do it "because it's there."

This book is the culmination of several decades of my own efforts to achieve success, not just once or in a singular avenue of life but as a matter of philosophy in all facets of life. There have, of course, been highs and lows and ebbs and flows and all the makings of a Hollywood film. Who knows, that might just be in the cards one day. Despite my age and my many accomplishments, I feel as though I am just now beginning to fulfill my true potential. (I'll wager many of you feel the same way.) What the future holds for me is just as bright, if not brighter, than the many days that have led me to this point. After all, a key hallmark of a true entrepreneur is unflagging optimism, even in the face of daunting odds.

For readers to appreciate the full context of this book, I highly recommend my first book, *Barefoot to Benefactor: My Life Story of Faith and Courage* (Post Hill Press, September 2021). Starting there will provide deeper insight into my personal metamorphosis and the driving forces that led to the development of the principles outlined herein.

It might also be helpful for readers to look over the Lenny Peters Foundation website (lennypetersfoundation.org) and see firsthand why these books truly matter. For as much as any one reader might obtain from their contents, so many more lives will benefit from the sale of each book. This includes orphaned children, the elderly, and the terminally ill. Our mission is to help care for and provide for those who cannot fend for themselves, and we are actively doing so across the world.

That mission is the driving force, the soul, that encouraged me to write this book and that remains my guiding principle. The first book and the work undertaken by the Lenny Peters Foundation underscore the philosophical and practical application of the principles outlined in this book.

As beneficial as these principles have been for my own life, I genuinely believe the same can be true for you as well, no matter your station in life or where you come from or what you might have endured.

My life is a blueprint: you can go as far as your ambition and grit will take you.

The 10 principles outlined in this book, if consistently applied with conviction and determination, can help you reach that form of "success" that works best for you. If nothing else, what you read in these next chapters will, I hope, inspire, inform, entertain, and encourage you to persevere and to see things through to the end. By applying these principles and molding them to coincide with your inherent abilities and talents, I have no doubt you will be equipped to succeed in tackling whatever ambition you hope to realize.

The fact that you are already thinking along these lines and are seeking resources such as this book to help you accomplish your goals is in itself a success. For starters, it means you have not given up. It means you are still seeking to improve, to refine your skills and thought processes, and to perhaps gain a different perspective than you have so far employed in your journey. As you will soon learn, that is exactly the mindset I had to adopt over the course of my own life and career such that I am now poised to share with you some of the things I learned along the way.

I have traveled the world extensively, become licensed to practice medicine on four continents, and broken bread with top echelon leaders of society and government in several nations, including U.S. presidents.

While I have achieved success in life as well as in business and I have been blessed with the means to serve my community, what I always come back to is what I might impart to my children and grandchildren, what sort of legacy I might leave behind. God has graced me with certain talents and abilities as He bestows on us all the traits that make us unique. Again, I offer a much more detailed account of my journey in that regard in the recently published autobiographical recounting of my career in medicine, commercial development, and finance, *Barefoot to Benefactor: My Life Story of Faith and Courage.*

With this book, however, I wanted to go a step further and offer a few key insights as to how over these many years I have considered tough decisions, taken bold risks, and rebounded from failures along the way. We all make mistakes, and we all face times in our lives when we must either adapt our plan or abandon a big idea. I am not one to easily abandon an idea in which I strongly believe, and so I have many times faced seemingly impossible odds and still managed to succeed, with the help of God.

A question I often receive at events or in private when speaking with others, particularly immigrants like myself, centers on how I managed to achieve all that I have. I rarely have time to answer such a broad question effectively, but with this book, I have managed to compile a list and whittle it down to the 10 or so chapters that, combined, do just that.

Curiosity is a godsend and, conversely, the incurious mind shackles us to a life of mediocrity. We must look beyond our own noses at the world around us, as well as to the past. Let us strive to look broadly at the world and learn the lessons of history.

Make no mistake, I do not place myself in the same category as any of the great figures identified or highlighted in this book. No, I decided early in the process of formulating the idea for this book that I would include historical examples and draw upon well-known figures whom I admire and whose decisions or triumphs or processes have in some way or another influenced my own.

To me, and I can only speak for myself, leadership is one quality among a litany of others one must possess to lead a successful life, whether in family matters and relationships, in business, or wherever applicable.

Consider, if you will, Thomas Jefferson, the writer, tinkerer, inventor, architect, agriculturalist, diplomat, and of course, the third President of the United States of America. Yes, his life choices are held to scrutiny in the context of today's cancel culture.

And yet, it is Jefferson to whom history attributes the writing of the Declaration of Independence, although there were certainly other contributors. I suppose it is probably due to my status as an immigrant who came to this country and loved it so that I became a citizen and created a life here, raised my family here, established my wealth and my legacy here, that I can say definitively the Declaration along with the Constitution and the Bill of Rights helped establish the greatest social experiment in the history of mankind, the United States of America.

Being an immigrant, I learned early on, and I share this with many people but particularly with fellow immigrants, that we must be the very best Americans we can be. I genuinely mean this; we must at all times be the best Americans we can possibly be. We must do so because so much is riding on our ability to make it here, to survive and to support our family and community, and to serve those in need here at home and around the world. It is true because, despite the founding documents and the many rights and opportunities enjoyed within its borders, there are those who believe the United States has a history of welcoming immigrants to its shores only to then shun them once they have arrived.

I must insist this is not true. What happens is that after arriving in America, immigrants are frequently held to higher standards and must work harder, longer, and smarter for acceptance. Immigrants are expected to either make it on our own or fail trying. The key idea is to try and not to despair of what is sometimes a clear-cut double-standard, one for immigrants and one for the native-born.

We do not yet live in a post-racial society. Sure, there is racism, there is prejudice, and there are historical and systemic barriers. To pretend these obstacles do not exist is to be untrue to ourselves and to each other. Yet these are just a few of the many obstacles any person must face in life, particularly when he or she has a big idea, a dream, or a passion he or she wishes to pursue.

For many of us, we experienced far worse in the countries from which we came, if not at least the same measure of resistance in one form or another. Otherwise, we would not have left our countries of origin.

In short, there are many reasons successful people continue to succeed, and there are many more reasons people who do not succeed never seem to do so. It is not, I can assure you, because of failure. Successful people fail. We fail en route to success as well as after achieving it. We fail more than those who don't succeed because no matter the outcome, we keep trying. I would argue that a certain degree of failure is not only normal for us but that it is good. There is a certain wisdom we gain from failure.

What sustains us is the fact that we have the drive, the fire in the belly, to get back up and keep going, and not just one time but many times, as many times as it takes until the next time becomes our time.

I will outline in this book what throughout my life and over the course of my career I have identified as my own *Peters' 10 Principles for Success.* This is not my entire playbook by which I run my life or businesses. Rather, these are the top qualities, attributes, and habits a person must possess, whether they come naturally or must be acquired and refined over time, to not only achieve success but to repeat it, sustain it, grow it, and pass it on.

For what is success if it does not propel our future generations to surpass us and become even better citizens of the world?

In 2018, I was asked to present the trophy to the winning team at a soccer tournament for which my company, Bethany Medical, was the key sponsor. The teams were amateur, of course, and comprised of immigrants from across the globe, each representing the nation from which they came. As it turned out the two final teams were of people from Sudan versus a team of South Korean immigrants. The Sudanese team proved the victor. I was not eager to present the trophy in front of a large crowd of people, many of whom I knew but most of whom were strangers. Yet as the head of the company that helped fund the event, I had the obligation to make the presentation; it was only right.

The night before I was to show up and present the trophy, I had an epiphany. I realized I had nothing to fear. The people in attendance were immigrants or friends of immigrants and, therefore, they were just like me. I did not realize, however, until I was before this sea of multi-colored, multicultural faces just how alike we all are.

I suppose many of the people involved with the tournament had heard my name or knew something about one of my companies or my various interests. When it came time for me to address the audience and present the team from Sudan with its trophy, I was not surprised that so many of them pointed at me or nudged a friend and made some comment to get their attention and focus on me. What surprised me was how interested many of these people were in my story, in how I had gotten to where I was, and the keys to my success. I admit I shared with so many people that day so many stories, tips, and tidbits that I have acquired over the years that I do not factually recall what I might have said to any of them. The crowd wanted to hear more. After the presentation, they tracked me down in small groups on the same soccer field, asking many more questions. I realized it would take a long time to answer even a few of them. I recall in that very moment, I decided I would write this book.

As you well know, 2020 brought with it a lot of unexpected challenges. A global pandemic coupled with political and social unrest and economic uncertainty makes for a challenging year; it offers no time to sit with one's thoughts and contemplate one's own success.

Late in the year, though, I was nearing the end of the previous book I have already mentioned. With it mostly written, I was spending time revising and editing it, and I decided that after the first of the new year, I would begin to write this book. What better time than just coming out of a period of chaos and hardship to equip people with a roadmap to success?

Particularly in my neck of the woods, High Point, North Carolina, and the surrounding Triad region that includes Greensboro and Winston-Salem, there is a hotbed of entrepreneurial activity right now, and I sensed that people on the rise or in transition might benefit from some of the wisdom and hard-learned lessons—more than I would like to admit—I have accumulated over my many years. And, frankly, none of us are promised tomorrow. So, I thought, what better time than the present to write down for my family and future generations of business leaders a few of the guiding principles by which I have lived, worked and, more often than not, succeeded.

I hope you enjoy both this and my earlier memoir, and you might one day apply the principles I set forth for you. If so, recommend it to a friend, and with all things in life, in business, and in general, I wish you the utmost success.

> "It is precisely in those moments when we are tested and tired that we must conjure up the energy and the willpower to think big, to overcome, and to persevere."

Lenny Peters, M.D.

High Point, N.C.

ACKNOWLEDGEMENTS

To my daughter, Elise Peters Carey, who taught me how to be strong and to charge forward in good times and bad times. You stood by me with unyielding support and encouragement, and it brought out the best in me. I have, over the years, been moved by your abilities and your confidence to grow as you work to continue my legacy.

To my son, Anthony Peters, for teaching me humility. Despite any milestone or accomplishment, you demonstrate time and again how to remain humble and treat everyone with respect. As you have shown to me often, the limelight is not always the best light.

To my daughter, Nicole Peters, you taught me how to love unconditionally. You revealed to me the wealth to be found in small gestures, particularly within our family, and how to care for one another. Whether with a kind word, a short visit, or remembering the small but important details of a gathering, you remind me that sometimes the smallest things matter most.

To my daughter, Shirin Peters, your strength is in facing adversity. Your ability to change and adapt to new situations and find new fronts while keeping focused on your mission has been a valuable lesson to me. I am proud of you for your accomplishments and the eight Bethany Medical clinics you have built in Manhattan.

Elise, Anthony, Nicole, and Shirin—I am proud of each of you and humbled to be your dad.

Lastly, I have been blessed to live and work on four of the six inhabitable continents. Throughout my journey, I have met many "Angels Without Wings" —people who unexpectedly and unbegrudgingly appeared in my path when I most needed them. These were ordinary people with extraordinary abilities. I am obliged to thank each of them for helping me through my journey from a young barefoot boy to a successful doctor, businessman, real estate developer, and benefactor.

Their names are too many to mention; I would be afraid to omit any one of them, although many of their angelic acts are recounted in my first book, *Barefoot to Benefactor: My Life Story of Faith and Courage.*

When I needed a hand from God, these souls appeared, and their gestures blessed me abundantly and lifted me to heights I do not deserve. Based on these experiences and others I have witnessed, I am convinced beyond a shadow of a doubt that angels without wings exist all around us; we have only to open our souls and our minds to receive them.

With all my love,

> **"It is not about how much you do, but how much
> love you put into what you do that counts."**
>
> MOTHER TERESA

SECTION I
EFFORT

"Success is dependent on effort."

SOPHOCLES

PRINCIPLE #1:

DO IT NOW!

"Only put off to tomorrow what
you are willing to die having left undone."
PABLO PICASSO

Do it now!

A core pillar of leadership excellence is decisiveness. Time is our most precious commodity. To quote Bishop Rosie O'Neal: "Procrastination is the arrogant assumption that God owes you another chance to do tomorrow what he gave you the chance to do today."

Amen.

Quick and accurate decision-making can make or break a leader, and it may mean the difference between being a successful person who on occasion has failed and one who fails to become successful.

Whether starting out in business or employing a new growth strategy, to be successful one must decide early on to move in a particular direction, to take a first step that will ultimately lead to another and then another. A leader decides to move with purpose, with a plan, and with a direction toward a series of short-and long-term goals that will carry the person or the business from Point A to Point B, typically within a given timeframe.

An associate of mine has two ways of referring to those who cannot act decisively. One is "analysis paralysis," where stasis results from overthinking a situation. His other phrase is "procrastination assassination," where ideas with enormous potential are simply "murdered" by needless foot-dragging.

There are various approaches a person can take when it comes to making decisions. Additionally, what may be a good decision-making process under one set of circumstances may not be viable under a different set of parameters. There may not be as much time or information available.

A person who hopes to be successful must cultivate a method by which, no matter the circumstances, he or she can be decisive when it matters. None of us are right 100 percent of the time, but successful people can learn to be correct an average of 80 percent of the time. This is done by compiling the best information available at the time, by looking as far down the road as possible at what might or might not happen if one course is chosen over another, and by gaining the confidence to pull the trigger and the willingness to live with the consequences. The popular way to express this is: don't let the pursuit of perfection be the enemy of the good.

That latter portion will get tested, and therefore it may be the most important aspect of decision making, particularly in business. Much like a professional athlete who loses a game or a general who is defeated in battle, leaders must remain resilient. If a decision is made that does not pan out as planned or is flat out incorrect, a leader must retain the confidence—that trust in himself or herself that 80 percent of the time their instincts are correct—or he or she will continue to fail again and again. In sports, it is said a quarterback must have a short memory. If he throws an interception, he had better not dwell on it the next time he holds the ball in his hands or he will never complete the next pass. The same logic applies in striving toward success. We can learn from our mistakes, but we also must learn to quickly get over them.

The default position of too many modern leaders is to kick the can down the road. Punt. Opt for job security over making a tough decision.

There is nothing more frustrating for a company than to have a leader who is indecisive.

And know this: if ever a person weighs the pros and cons and charts the potential outcomes of a pending decision, and then chooses *not* to follow up with action, a decision has still been made. Often, opting not to evaluate the pros and cons [Do It Now] can prove more disastrous than having chosen a wrong course of action. Adjustments can be made to a plan once in motion, but hesitation or procrastination results in death by a thousand cuts. Opportunities can be missed, time and money wasted, and confidence lost in the ability of the one who was supposed to lead.

Whether as the head of a family, a CEO of a company, or a leader in one's community, to be unwilling to act decisively with the best information available at the time is to leave everyone who is to follow you exposed to potential negative outcomes. Advantages will be ceded; opportunities will be overlooked.

The qualities others see in us are often manifestations of our adopted philosophies. For example, what is a person's life? A person's life is made up of time. When we run out of time, we are no longer here. When a person talks about wanting to live longer, what he or she means is there is a desire to better use time, and time in that sense reflects life. So "do it now" saves time and in a way prolongs life.

Having said that, we all have a tendency from which none of us is excluded. It is human nature to say, "Let's do it tomorrow." Risk tolerance varies from person to person. And so, depending on the decision looming or the scope of the plan waiting to be executed, hesitation may prove fatal. I have encountered this many times throughout my professional career, and when others have asked me, then or now, how I was able to move while others continued to weigh options and ponder their positions, my answer is always the same.

I look at the worst possible outcome and determine whether I can survive it. By survive, I mean in all possible ways: physically, financially, emotionally. If so, I move ahead. If not, I will choose another option. But to stand by or hem and haw, wringing my hands and continually asking for more information or for better options to be presented, I am only wasting time and forfeiting all competitive advantage.

Procrastination is the enemy of success.

That is not to say one ought to be impulsive. It is important to have as much information as can be gathered and to consider ahead of time potential outcomes of the decision being faced. Options should be presented, evaluated and, if plausible, considered in depth. Still, one must safeguard against analysis paralysis.

Yes, we can wait briefly to gather more information or to evaluate our plans a little farther down the line, but that can be an endless journey. Overwhelming ourselves with too much information can lead us to make the wrong decision. This brings us back to the 80/20 rule, meaning a successful person should aim to be right about 80 percent of the time. One who finds himself or herself being proven right 100 percent of the time is one who is waiting around too long, deciding only in hindsight after the outcome has been determined. This is someone not taking enough chances and not making timely, efficient decisions.

Overall, a successful person learns to assess a situation as quickly as possible and tries to act on things as early as is reasonable. There will always be some element of risk, but if we look throughout history, some of the toughest decisions that have been made held not only thousands of lives in the balance, but also the future of what the world might look like if all was lost.

Here's a historical perspective that illustrates my point. The 16th President of the United States, Abraham Lincoln, led the nation through its darkest time. At the outset of the Civil War, Lincoln selected the right man to lead the Union's military forces and get the nation's standing army into fighting shape. The number of U.S. troops had dwindled since the Mexican-American War, and so too had the American forces' readiness to fight. Gen. George McClellan, historians largely agree, was the right man to get the troops facing front and marching in step again. It was, however, his lack of will to fight and to pursue the enemy that led to many early clashes with Lincoln over how the war was being conducted.[1]

Lincoln, who was using all his political capital and diplomatic prowess to hold together the public's resolve to preserve the nation, was faced with a decision: keep the celebrated Gen. McClellan in place or find someone else to lead the Union to victory. The president made a decision that was unpopular at the time. But history proves he made the right choice. McClellan might never have turned on the offensive. It is true, Lincoln changed generals a few more times before finally selecting Gen.

---

1 "Order Relieving General G.B. McClellan and Making Other Changes." Abraham Lincoln, 1826; *Abraham Lincoln: Complete Works, Comprising His Speeches, Letters, State Papers, and Miscellaneous Writings,* eds. John G. Nicolay and John Hay, 1894.

Ulysses S. Grant. But Grant led Union forces in the successful campaign at Vicksburg along the Mississippi River, which ultimately boxed in Confederate General Robert E. Lee at Appomattox Courthouse in Virginia and brought the deadliest conflict in U.S. history to a close.

Yet the president would never have been able to position Grant and the rest of the Union Army for success if he had wavered in the years before and not made the first decision to replace McClellan.

"(Time) cannot and must not be ignored," Abraham Lincoln, wrote to McClellan in October 1862. "If we never try, we shall never succeed."

Next example: Churchill. In 1940, less than six weeks into his role as British Prime Minister, Winston Churchill made the still-controversial decision to do something otherwise unthinkable. At the time, however, he must have felt he was left no other viable choice than to act. It was a difficult decision that might heavily influence the outcome of World War II.

With the luxury of 20/20 hindsight, we know today that Churchill emerged from World War II as one of the greatest world leaders in modern history, both for his decisions regarding the management of the war and his resolve in guiding the people of Britain through the Blitz, the devastating bombing campaign by the German Luftwaffe that left much of London in ruins and killed thousands of civilians. Yet Churchill's position in his own time as well as in the annals of history was not so certain at the time these events unfolded.

France's fleet of naval warships was in danger of being taken over by the Germans after the fall of Paris.[2] Despite his pleas to the U.S. for

---

2   "Secrets of the Dead: Churchill's Deadly Decision," Richard Bond, Furnace Ltd., PBS, 2010.

assistance, President Franklin D. Roosevelt had yet to see enough out of the British not to think any U.S. Navy ships handed over to the U.K. forces would eventually meet the same fate and be used later by the Germans to repel any future U.S. Naval campaign against the Axis. America continued to withhold its assistance.

This left Churchill with one choice, demand the French navy willingly turn over its ships to the British or take them by force. The French refused his demand, allowing a deadline set by Churchill to come and go. Churchill, in turn, ordered his forces to attack the British ally and seize or sink the French fleet. His order was carried out, and more than 1,300 French sailors were killed.

The decisive move accomplished two things which ultimately proved pivotal to the Allied Forces' later victory. It kept the French fleet out of the hands of the Nazis, and it gave Roosevelt the confidence he needed that Britain was in the fight to win, and so the U.S. handed over 50 warships to the British to help keep the U.K. from being invaded and to stay in the war.

In the first example, Lincoln had the advantage of time. He made several attempts over many weeks and months to urge McClellan to move and to pursue the enemy. The general did not comply. Over time, the data Lincoln was confronted with did not support his plan for success, so he was forced to abandon it and reassess.

In the second scenario, what seemed like it might take months to determine was instead decided in a few days. After weeks of being refused by Roosevelt and ultimately rebuffed by the French, Churchill had only hours to decide and act. Had he hesitated, the French fleet and ultimately Britain might very well have fallen to the Nazis, Britain might have been lost, and the outcome of the war and the future of the world compromised.

These wartime examples are indicative, on a much larger scale of course, of the consequences of tough decisions having to be made, decisions whose outcomes were by no means assured, to achieve immediate goals and stave off ultimate defeat. In business, the consequences of one decision or another may not result in the deaths of thousands of people but could instead mean the loss of as many jobs. Decisiveness could perhaps mean the difference between expanding the business and seeing it go under.

In terms of my own life-story, I have faced many decisions that could only have been guided by faith and a plan God held for me. These choices eventually brought me 8,200 miles, from Kerala, in southwest India near the Arabian Sea, to High Point, North Carolina, where I built my fortune as well as my family's legacy over the last 35 years.

I have been a doctor on four continents, a leader in banking and in commercial real estate, as well as in community development and philanthropy. None of this would have been possible if I had wavered at any moment in my decisiveness along the way.

Allow me to explain.

I left my home, a small village in India with no running water or electricity, at the age of 14. After attending pre-med and medical school, I again decided to take an uncharted path and moved to the U.K., where I knew not a living soul, to practice medicine and advance my career. A perhaps safer, more traditional path had been laid out for me. Remain in India. Agree to an arranged marriage, as was the custom. Practice medicine and become a local leader in my native region of Kerala.

Sounds OK, but I had bigger ambitions, and I felt called to move about the world. So, despite my fears, as well as a profound lack of money and the requisite network of contacts to help me, I set off for London.

God has placed many angels in my life, and people along my journey have seemed to spring up at just the moment I needed them with just the right number of resources I needed, no more, no less. The years passed, and I continued to follow my instincts. I traveled first to Nigeria for a year, and then on to the United States, where I studied at the University of Pittsburgh.

Each new country required a repeat of the residency process in that nation to be permitted to practice medicine. It takes a lot of work and discipline to become a doctor, let alone to do so four times in different corners of the world.

It might seem easy today for me to describe the thought processes by which I made the decision each time, when and where I would then go, and what I might do when I got there. The anxiety nearly overwhelmed the mind of the 14-year-old boy who was me, an earnest yet provincial future global citizen who had not seen much beyond his own village. The 24-year-old, newly accredited doctor who had not practiced medicine in a major metropolitan hospital setting was similarly challenged.

How did I overcome these professional and personal hurdles? I put in the effort to analyze the pros and cons, and then make the tough choices. To this day, when faced with a decision that I absolutely must make, whether regarding my life, my family, or in business, I always think, "What is the worst that can happen? Will I survive if I make this decision?"

If the answer is, "Yes, this is a doable choice," that seems to be the best choice, and I make it. If the very worst outcome I can imagine is something I can still deal with, after reviewing all my options, and if I feel comfortable moving ahead, I do so. I take that leap of faith.

I am an options-oriented man. If I do not know what the options are, I ask. I confer with my colleagues, my team, my family, and then I choose an option. I may wait a day; I may think about it a bit longer.

To some, my approach might sound a bit like "ready…fire…aim." Not really, though. For there is a chasm between shooting from the hip and waiting too long to decide upon the optimal course of action, the one with what you know—in your heart of hearts—has the highest chance of success.

My process is not easy, for life is difficult and there are sometimes daunting societal circumstances that impact our decision-making process.

Take systemic racism as one very big example. I'll tell you a story. Not long after coming to North Carolina to practice as a gastroenterologist and conduct research at the University of Wake Forest, I decided I wanted to own my own practice. I was not yet the savviest of businessmen, although I had a modicum of success in financial matters and successfully managed ventures at my various stops around the world.

But back to North Carolina. I steadily built a small real estate portfolio through the acquisition of a few rental properties. My wealth and resources grew and yet purchasing and running my own practice was a huge step. This was going to be my business, alone, and there would be no one above or beside me to help make the decisions.

Daily life in the mid-80s, in the American South, was a challenge for me, an immigrant with dark skin and a thick Indian accent. Racism persisted despite the advances made since the days of Jim Crow. There was the ever-present reality that, at any time on any given day, some or all the local white doctors—my conduit for patient referrals—might choose to pinch their pipeline of patients to me for consults and for treatment. If that had happened, my business would have dried up and I might have gone bankrupt.

Furthermore, there also seemed to be on the horizon another threat to my independent practice, which ultimately came to bear for those around me. Independent practitioners would soon be subsumed by the kudzu-like growth of powerful health systems in the area, due to rising costs of health care and narrowing legislation and liabilities such as the growing cost of malpractice insurance and other constraints. It was becoming harder for a sole practitioner to remain viable.

For both of these reasons, I had to consider my options.

I knew I did not want to work for someone else. I also knew I did not want to move again. I now had a family, and we had found a home in the community of High Point that we liked, and we wanted to stay there and grow. I decided to open my multi-specialty practice where I could see patients under the umbrella of primary care, and if a gastroenterology consult were needed, patients from my own practice would only have to go as far as the next room.

So many of my fellow doctors told me I was crazy. They laughed at me, but I could see what many of them could not. Either that, or I had the confidence to act on what I saw inevitably coming for us all, consolidation. I knew I could very well go bankrupt if my patient base were taken from me, but I knew I would not go broke by opening a multi-specialty practice and adding to my own patient base.

And I was right.

In 1987, I put together a team and started Bethany Medical Center. Besides my detractors, I had to contend with my own self-doubt. I am not immune, but I do not suffer from doubt the way others might, perhaps because I am a doctor. I know that if you have a theory in science, you test the theory to see if you can reproduce the expected result. In business, the approach is the same (or should be).

That is, if you have an idea, you test it. You evaluate what works and what does not. You then modify the approach in favor of what works, and you repeat the process. I did not linger in doubt because as we tested the theory that Bethany Medical Center would be successful, we found out we were right.

In the short term, the practice was soon up and running, and every day we added new patients. The practice very quickly grew, and I began to hire more providers, more nurses and nurse practitioners, more physician's assistants, and staff. When that rapid growth takes place and you see what you can build, that self-doubt goes away. We added locations and built buildings to house our ever-growing family of care providers and patients.

Self-doubt is a defense mechanism, but it can also be an important counterweight that prevents gross miscalculations and mistakes. It keeps you engaged as you test your theories and evaluate results. In that way, when you do identify success, you can build out your infrastructure to support the growth.

Today, with 15 locations across the region known as the Triad—these are the cities of Greensboro, Winston-Salem, and High Point—as well as in Wilkesboro, Mount Airy, and Kernersville, we now see more than 1,100 patients per day. We dropped the "Center" from the name and now Bethany Medical is the largest independent practice in the region, and one of the only few remaining practices that is wholly independently owned, not affiliated with a hospital or health system.

I am quite proud of what my team and I were able to accomplish. We put in the effort, and it paid off for ourselves and our patients.

And I take subtle satisfaction as I recall how those other doctors and providers laughed at me so many years ago. I did not give in to fear or doubt. I trusted the data, looked deep within myself, and saw that what I was doing was right. My detractors were not "wrong" at the time; they simply saw things differently. I believe they were content with the short-term income they were receiving, and I understood that.

What they did *not* see was the long-term perspective, as I could. My situation analysis made it clear: my profession was and still is in transition, and I was on shaky ground. I would soon need more stability to stay afloat and to grow.

So, I let them laugh at me, but I said to them, "You are laughing now, but I will have the last laugh."

And I was right.

> **"Procrastination is the thief of time; collar him."**
> **CHARLES DICKENS**

PRINCIPLE #1 TAKEAWAYS

- Don't let the pursuit of perfection be the enemy of the good.
- If you're right 80 percent of the time, congratulations.
- Remain resilient in the face of adversity.
- *Not* making a decision is, in fact, a decision.
- Do not succumb to "analysis paralysis" or "procrastination assassination." Weigh your options and then act!

PRINCIPLE #2:

BE HONEST WITH OURSELVES

"There are two ways to be fooled.
One is to believe what isn't true; the other
is to refuse to believe what is true."
SOREN KIERKEGAARD

Life has revealed certain elemental truths to me. In poker, a flush beats a straight. Facts can be cruel, but they outweigh opinions. And it takes guts to face and defeat tough truths if we are to give our best effort.

There are times we encounter facts that we do not like. Something we *believe* is true might be proven to be untrue, or vice versa. This can cause our brains to play tricks on us. Each of us has a comfort zone, which makes existing in this world more tolerable.

Defense mechanisms, which I touched upon in the previous chapter, help us cope with life's pain. These are psychological strategies unconsciously used to protect ourselves from anxiety caused by difficult thoughts and feelings. Such techniques include denial, rationalization, and repression.

We find in life what makes us most comfortable. In this way, we choose the people we enjoy being around, the places we live and visit, and the sources of information we believe.

Yet when something fails to fit into our comfort zone, it is human nature to develop selective hearing. We might think we know best, or we can simply say to ourselves, "I do not *feel* like that is true."

Unfortunately, feelings and facts are not always in congruence. If we wish to be successful or to sustain the success we are already achieving, we must be honest with ourselves.

This takes remarkable effort.

It can become easy to deceive ourselves into thinking we are the ones who know better, *our* decisions are always the right decisions, *and our* methods are the best methods. These are partly our ego and partly our cognitive dissonance forcing a detour from the path of success onto the back roads of isolation and alienation. How can one be successful in a relationship or a family setting if he or she tunes everyone else out and refuses to hear or understand where the other people involved are coming from or what they might be going through? It is unsustainable. And the same is true in business.

We must be adaptable and open to new information, new data, evolving technology, and innovation and market disruptions. The Covid-19 pandemic disrupted global business on all fronts, from supply chain and manufacturing to the way the world uses virtual data and the way we get our food and visit with loved ones.

There are companies that turned this crisis into opportunity, and despite all the negativity, the death and illness and dark days of quarantine and government-imposed restrictions, these businesses turned a profit. Other businesses were built as a result of the pandemic, while many existing firms executed deft pivots to make new products geared toward battling the virus and therefore prospered in ways that otherwise might never have been possible.

Telehealth in the medical industry, and video conferencing platforms such as Zoom and Microsoft Teams took off. During the crisis and beyond it, doctors who once found it difficult to keep tabs on patients in remote or rural settings and patients with limited access to hospitals and clinics due to transportation or mobility issues connected virtually, meeting screen-to-screen rather than face-to-face. How many chronic illnesses might be better treated with more regular contact between providers and patients utilizing this technology?

Virtual calls and virtual private networks (VPNs) existed long before Covid-19 forced so many industries to adopt work-from-home capabilities. Yet look how much money companies have learned can be saved on travel, office space, and in-person events moved to the virtual platform space? Sure, we absolutely need to return in some facet to the in-person practices of doing business and being social. Global commerce depends on it, as does society in general. Yet there are now more readily accepted cost-saving measures that can be employed where managers and executives deem feasible. Prior to 2020-21, widespread use of such platforms would have been dismissed out of hand.

Admittedly, some leaders perfected their ostrich imitations and kept their heads firmly in the sand, oblivious to hard truths. The good news is that others did not waste time lying to themselves, whining that "someone" or "the world" was out to get them or, perhaps worse, that their businesses were somehow immune to world events. No, these savvy CEOs and leaders saw the world landscape as it was, anticipated changes, and decided to act quickly and decisively. They saw what was possible rather than what was being made impossible. That is precisely what we each must learn to do. And we can start by working proactively in our minds to recognize the boundaries of our comfort zones, face the hard truths and, when it comes time to make decisions, have the courage to overrun those self-imposed borders.

There are simple questions we can ask ourselves when faced with an opportunity to lie to ourselves. We might even ask those around us whom we trust, an executive board or a team member, a co-founder or even our spouse or significant other.

And what do we ask? "What are the facts?" "What rock do we stand on?"

Making the effort to face reality requires reintroducing ourselves to our inner gyroscope and compass. We must remain steady in our search for True North.

To know which direction is best, we must first assess our starting position and, next, plot a course that will lead our organization to the desired position. If we are not being honest with ourselves, whether about our abilities or inabilities, the state of the industry, or of the world, will we ever really get from Point A to Point B or will we fail? Perhaps we will only swim in circles and waste time, neither failing nor growing. Stagnation is never a desirable outcome.

This takes us back to our individual comfort zones and a showdown with our defense mechanisms, perhaps in the form of a self-audit. Take stock of the flaws within ourselves, characteristics we know deep down we can improve upon, yet we do not want to address. Why? Because these are uncomfortable, inconvenient truths. "Mirror, mirror on the wall" and all that.

If I look around, whether in the office or at home, and I do not like what I see, things are trending negatively and morale is down or numbers are down or we are not communicating as openly and lovingly as we once had, I must first look in the mirror. Am I being honest with myself? What are my shortcomings? How might I improve?

What have I done to address it? How have I changed since I last looked around and was pleased? Is my behavior or attitude different? Am I causing this, or if not, how might I change anyway to be better suited to lead us out of this period of difficulty?

It cannot always be a laundry list of demands placed on others and pounding one's fist on the table and pointing the finger down the line. If we want to be celebrated for our successes, we must first be accountable for our failures, to ourselves and others, and this requires that we be brutally honest with ourselves.

Here is a recent example. Aeronautics giant Boeing having to ground the entire fleet of its new model 737 Max commercial aircraft in 2019 due to mechanical issues following two fatal crashes that year is a prime example. The company took on an estimated nearly $20 billion in losses, possibly more by this printing, according to a CNN report in March of 2020.[3]

Boeing took ownership of its failures in the manufacturing process, grounded the fleet, and corrected the problem despite the great cost incurred. Of course, the company could not have escaped taking some action. The Federal Aviation Administration and other regulatory bodies exist to ensure passenger safety and compliance with certain criteria before aircraft can resume flight after such an instance. Still, Boeing accepted its responsibility and continues to work with regulators, has established a $100 million compensation fund for the families of victims, and has

---

3   "The Cost of the Boeing 737 Max Crisis: $18.7 Billion and counting." Chris Isadore; *CNN Business*, March 10, 2020.

endured ceding a competitive advantage to its rivals during a time when other companies' aircraft continued to fly.

I hope not to give the impression I am overlooking the loss of life in this example. I am not. I am saying that when tragedy strikes, even in less costly instances, we should all hold ourselves accountable. Take ownership. Understand we are leading God's team, not our own.

That's Boeing's story. Here's mine. Believe me, there have been many, many times where I have had to take a spoonful or two of the bitter taste of self-realization. Leaders are often categorized as "Alphas" or "Type A" personalities. Sure, it is necessary to have confidence and to be firm in one's convictions if one is to lead and to attain success. But we are the ones often too bullheaded to heed the advice of others.

This was around the time of my second divorce. After more than two decades of marriage, raising our four children and building our business portfolio together, my ex-wife and I realized we had grown apart. We were living very different lives and so, amicably, we decided to split. That took a degree of self-honesty on both our parts, certainly. Still, in the aftermath of the divorce I went astray from my own best interest.

I found myself living alone in an apartment again for the first time since I was a young man. With time, I will admit, a mixture of loneliness and boredom drove me to seek diversion, so I ventured out into the nightlife of downtown Greensboro, North Carolina. What I found enticed me, not only in the thrill of meeting and being around so many people mingling and having a good time, but also in the sense of new opportunities.

I met the owner of one of Greensboro's hottest nightclubs at the time, a place called Heaven. In short, within weeks of my first visit, I became a regular and purchased the building as well as the business itself from the owner. With a couple of partners, I went full tilt into the entertainment industry, not exactly one of my core competencies.

I had managers and bartenders and a full staff to run the place, and after a few minor changes to the décor and ambiance, the nightclub became even more upscale, more spectacular. I enjoyed the attention that came along with being the owner of the most popular nightclub in town: the VIP treatment, the clamoring for my attention, and also the money that rolled in.

After a year or two, though, I grew physically tired and emotionally weary. I realized I was spending so much of my energy and time on something that, although exciting and lucrative, left me feeling quite empty and unfulfilled. I am a healer, first and foremost. And I am a man of faith.

While I did not take part in any activities that might besmirch my character as a doctor and a prominent figure in the community or compromise my faith, I had to admit I was not serving my true purpose by devoting so much to the entertainment industry. The nightlife was a great escape, but it was not my calling. I had to stop lying to myself and admit I was filling an empty-nester void after my divorce and my children had all gone off to college and begun their lives outside of our family home. It was time to return to what motivated me and what not only draws the best out of me but also best fulfills my life and gives me purpose, being a doctor and helping the people around me. I have been happier, and my business has grown exponentially ever since.

There are examples throughout history as well where not only individuals, but entire nations have been swayed and led into wars or periods of unrest because of the human mind's ability to deceive itself.

The people of Germany in the 1930s and '40s fell victim to this very human tendency, believing their government was restoring national pride and removing a societal albatross from around its neck by sweeping segments of the population into ghettos and later concentration camps. Few knew the extent of what was taking place, and the full scope of the atrocities committed did not come to light for most until the end of the Second World War.

Yet, along the way people were fed information, witnessed deplorable acts, and stood by as various groups, particularly the Jewish people but also non-whites, homosexuals, the disabled, and countless other subsets of the population were humiliated, ostracized, financially ruined, and ultimately rounded up and massacred in a genocidal campaign.

The blame extends beyond the borders of Nazi Germany and beyond the reach of the Third Reich. Here in America, anti-Semitism kept the U.S. from accepting European refugees of the Jewish faith. One such account, which took place in 1939 and was retold in the *Miami Herald* as recently as 2019, saw both Cuba and the U.S. refuse port to a ship filled with German-Jewish refugees. In what became known as the Voyage of the Damned, the S.S. St. Louis and its more than 900 passengers were forced to return to Europe after fleeing the Nazis and subsequently being refused at ports in both Havana and Miami. The ship sailed to Hamburg, Germany, where upwards of 250 Jewish passengers were reportedly killed.[4]

The bitter taste left on the tongue of the American people from the Great War, later known as World War I, kept the U.S. out of World War II for longer than perhaps it would have otherwise. President Roosevelt was not inclined to enter the war, not because the Yanks did not have the stomach for it; there simply was not the incentive to sacrifice thousands of American lives in what seemed at the time a European problem, largely because the full extent of what Adolf Hitler and the Nazi Party were engaging in was not yet known.

---

4   "The Time Havana and Miami wouldn't let a ship dock amid war. It was a deadly decision," Miami Herald Archives; 2017. Miamiherald.com

History has proven, though, that there were numerous times when either the German people or the Allied Powers could and should have interceded, which may very well have staved off some of the horrific outcomes of that period. The ability to convince ourselves that what we are seeing and hearing is not real or is exaggerated or perhaps necessary when of course we know it ought never be permitted was through a series of epic failures, magnified across the globe. So many heads buried in the sand refused to look up and see the truth before them.

A more recent example might resonate more with the current generation. Many of us need not look to the history books but only recall in our own minds the feelings of desperation, mistrust, and a bloodthirst for revenge following the attacks on September 11, 2001. Yet, what began as a mission to root out terrorism where it lived and trained and recruited its martyrs in the desert mountain regions of Afghanistan and Pakistan was soon redirected to an invasion of Iraq by the U.S. military on the premise that then-leader and dictator Saddam Hussein was developing and harboring weapons of mass destruction.

Because chemical weapons had been used in the 1980s in the Iraq-Iran war, as well as by Iraq on a subset of its people, a minority population known as the Kurds, it was expected that Hussein still possessed and might be inclined to use chemical or biological weapons against the U.S. or Coalition forces operating in the region during the so-called War on Terror.

Then-Secretary of State, former U.S. Army General Colin Powell famously delivered a speech before the United Nations in February 2003, seeking to convince the world's governments that intelligence reports from the U.S. Central Intelligence Agency, the National Security Administration, and a dozen other intel-gathering agencies all pointed to the existence of a cache of chemical weapons or sites busy in the development of such weapons. His mission achieved, the U.N. backed the U.S. in its attack on

Iraq, ultimately deposing Hussein and his Ba'ath Party and destabilizing the Iraqi government.

Years later, after knocking out the Hussein administration and leaving the Iraqi army and most of the nation's institutions without a plan to rebuild or safely extract U.S. and U.N. coalition forces after the fall of Baghdad, those who had banked on the intelligence reports being accurate were forced to accept the fact that they had been wrong. There were no chemical weapons in storage or in development found in Iraq.

The entire war was fought and executed under false pretenses. It was the willingness of the U.S. government, and frankly, the people, to be convinced that what they suspected was true. It was not, and that willingness to believe an idea without factual evidence led to what became the longest continuous foreign war (2003 to 2021) in American history, the decades-long campaign in Iraq and Afghanistan.

In countless interviews since, Powell has admitted to being wrong at the time of his U.N. address, and to being upset at the fact that while he pushed to have three and four sources supporting the data the government was poised to act upon, he was forced to go ahead when there was no such verification.

"I was disturbed but not panicked, because it all came out of the National Intelligence Estimate, NIE," Powell said to FRONTLINE's Jim Gilmore in 2016, during an interview ahead of the documentary, *The Secret History of ISIS.*[5]

"The [NIE] had been given the previous fall to the Congress; they're the ones who asked for it and they're the ones who got it. And all the

---

5   "Colin Powell: U.N. Speech 'Was a Great Intelligence Failure.'" Jason M. Breslow; May 2016; PBS; pbs.org

information about weapons of mass destruction as the intelligence community analyzed it was in that NIE."

It should be stated here that Powell's address came four months after the U.S. Congress voted to approve the military action proposed by the Bush Administration, and what was set in motion would most likely have taken place with or without Powell's involvement. Powell famously told Bush, "If you break it, you own it," regarding the potential for destabilizing the Iraqi government, which he later explained meant that if the U.S. went in and took out Hussein and his ruling party, then America would be responsible for whatever government it helped erect in its place, for better or worse.

Powell left his position at the end of President George W. Bush's first term, nearly three months following the President's re-election.

Today there is so much divisiveness in our culture, so many who view those who do not share their belief structure as enemies. Yet time and time again, we fail to put in the effort and have the emotional strength to be honest with ourselves.

We blame the shortcomings of others for the strain on our society. Income inequality exists and continues to grow, with profound impact on the less fortunate. Instead, we blame problems on certain races, or ethnicities, or religions. A person is lazy? Here is the hard truth: a demographic generationally marginalized by repressive laws and denied opportunities because of pervasive stereotypes and lack of access to quality education and access to capital cannot be simply dismissed as a group of lazy individuals.

I believe in our better angels; we might not like to admit it, but we know better. I know we do.

Women are as capable as their male counterparts. My own daughter is now the president of our entire portfolio of businesses. I would not have handed over our family's legacy to her simply because she is my daughter. Were she incapable in the slightest, to do so would have meant to jeopardize all of the wealth and progress I have accrued over the years, for my children and grandchildren. My trust in her is an example of the value I place on her ability to step into a leadership role overseeing a complex business organization at such a young age.

At a time when there is so much talk of diversity, equity, and inclusion, of fair and equal access, breaking of glass ceilings, and the breaking down of institutional racism and barriers to social and economic equality, there is also such violence and unrest and animosity in our politics and on our streets. We must ask ourselves: are we talking too much and doing too little? Are we really doing enough? Is what we are not doing a hindrance to change?

Are we afraid to look into that mirror on the wall, afraid to confront elemental truths?

We who have been blessed with the means and the experience in getting things done must answer when called upon to serve our communities. We must make contributions and donations to charities that help our communities. Consider starting and managing our own charitable foundations and creating access and opportunity where there is none, not because we seek to have our names on buildings or in the news, although there is nothing wrong with that if it arises out of the process.

We were born to manifest the glory of God that is within us. Not just some of us, but in all of us. As we allow our light to shine, we must give each other permission to do the same. It is OK to talk about your accomplishments or brand your companies with your name because those are all gifts from God or the Universe. By doing so, you are glorifying the blessings you have received and asking others to do the same. None of us can take our wealth with us.

No, we must tell ourselves the truth, that for all our inherent or God-granted abilities and skills, we are lucky. We have been afforded opportunities which others have not, and we have managed to find a way where others did not.

I do not suppose any of us take sole responsibility for the plights of others or the historical blights on society that continue today. Nor should we rely solely on the government or elected officials to shoulder the blame and create solutions. Rather, I am suggesting that we are each failing to be honest with ourselves if we do not see the opportunity in our communities to reinvest some of our financial and intellectual wealth to improve the lives and conditions of those around us.

> **"If you want to be successful, you must respect one rule: never lie to yourself."**
>
> PAULO COELHO

PRINCIPLE #2 TAKEAWAYS

- Face the hard truths and act accordingly; don't be an ostrich.
- Rely on your inner gyroscope and compass to seek balance and your True North.
- Take periodic self-audits to dust off "the mirror on the wall."
- Think about the last time you veered from your True North. How did it make you feel? How did you correct your course?

PRINCIPLE #3:

FIND A WAY

"Never give up on something that you can't go a day
without thinking about."
WINSTON CHURCHILL

From ancient fables to classic literature and modern-day Hollywood films, those tales which endure are replete with stories of heroes who "beat the odds."

Unfortunately, in business and many other facets of life, the proverbial "cutting room floor" is littered with stories of those who folded under pressure, who edited themselves out of their own success stories because they did not muster the resolve to push forward. These people quit when the going got tough because they did not possess the will to succeed.

Very often we hear the sentence, "Where there is a will, there is a way."

I would like to see more people put those words into practice. We must be strong-willed. Unfortunately, it is in too many people's nature to find excuses or to give up prior to investing enough effort into something they say is their dream.

For instance, one might say to oneself, "I am not smart enough." I challenge anyone to seek out some of the successful people around them and attempt to convince them they are not smart enough to achieve their goals. They may confess to having for a time held the same momentary doubt or to having run into obstacles while trying to find a way. Still, I guarantee the successful person would then begin to describe how he or she persevered, adapted an existing plan into a better one, and perhaps sought out resources to gain additional knowledge and then applied it to obtain their respective goals.

It is easy to see another person's success and rationalize that the person must have had it easier than we do. Or one might look and say that the successful person had advantages or abilities beyond our own. This is another lie we tell ourselves. The truth is there is a way to obtain any goal or to overcome any obstacle, yet it is seldom the first method tried or the easiest path chosen that will lead to the desired accomplishment.

Far be it from me to dismiss anyone's real challenges in life. There are many challenges universal to us all and there are others which are unique to our differences, for example, race, religion, gender, socioeconomic status, or geography. I do not diminish these very real barriers.

Nor do I permit them to deter me.

I can only draw on my experiences and observations throughout my life and tell you that while I have run across many of these issues at various points along my journey, I have had to acknowledge them, confront them, and overcome them. This is what is required to succeed. If the desire is strong, the person will find a way. If the primary path is not open to that person, he or she must find another way.

In many instances along my own path, I have had to find another way, and often I have done so by finding what I like to call a side door or a back door.

Growing up a minority Christian in India may have given me an advantage, as opposed to someone who has always lived within the majority. As I have said, I grew up very poor, without running water or electricity, or shoes for that matter. We did not miss what we did not have, but we learned to work hard and take every gift from God as a blessing and nothing for granted.

I also was darker-skinned than my siblings and many of my fellow students in school. It may surprise many Americans but, yes, this is also an issue in other countries. My older brother, for example, was fairer-skinned and much more athletic than I was as a boy. He was favored more and received more attention than I for these reasons, which led me to harbor a lot of resentment toward him in my early childhood.

Later, I would get over that when he and others around us gained respect for my intellect and my inclination to always help others. Also, we were Christians in a largely Hindu and Muslim society. Our faith was in the minority—only about five percent of the population were Christians—and there were many instances where this proved an obstacle in life, including the limitations in our career choices. It dashed our hopes to win or be appointed to political office and lowered our economic ceiling.

India was at the time a socialist country with a democratically elected government. Yet, because the country was 70 percent Hindu, it was unlikely the majority would elect minority Christians. I would never have had a great opportunity there, but I also knew that I could not hang my head or think too long about how I felt about things being this way. There was no time. I had to do the things I needed to do to get where I wanted to go, or I would not get there. I was not willing to settle for mediocrity or a humdrum "average" life. I developed a strong will and took it as a challenge to always see past the front door, my term for the unobstructed pathways of those in the majority.

Because I grew up this way, I learned to assess situations from the outset, to know right away whether there was a side door or a back door. For example, I knew I could not afford to go to England to practice medicine, which was my dream. I did not want to stay in India and lead the traditional life that was expected of me. I had higher ambitions.

Yet, the front door was closed to me because I had no money, I had no family member already living in England who could act as my sponsor, which was required, and I had no job there waiting for me. I needed to find a side door.

The side door came in the form of a friend whose father lived in London and worked as a ticket collector for the British Rail. Without my asking him to, this friend offered to see if his father would sponsor me, to which he happily agreed. He even sent me a small sum of money for necessities along the trip and when I reached London, he allowed me to stay with him in his very humble flat until I was able to take the required tests to be allowed to practice medicine in the U.K. and find a job.

Of course, I also had to borrow money from my extended family to pay for the plane ticket, which cost more than I had ever seen at that point in my life, with the solemn promise to pay the money back as soon as I could. I did that. Yet without the help from these other people, whom I have come to call the angels placed in my life by God, I would not have been able to begin my journey, which ultimately led me to where I am today.

The other requirement throughout this process has been, for me, maintaining a strong faith. I needed a vast reserve of courage to ask my family for a loan, fly alone to England to meet and stay with a man whom I had never met, and seek a job as an immigrant doctor in a foreign country with no guarantee I would be hired.

This took faith and prayer. From prayers, I gained courage, and with that came determination. If these people believed in me and would go out of their way for me, then I would believe in myself as well, and I would go out of my way, however difficult or uncomfortable it might be, to succeed and pay them back.

Today, people often ask me how I know which path to take. Sure, if the front door is closed to you, seek a side door or a back door. Still, how does one know *which* door to take in a particular instance? After all, we are all different and have different tolerances for risk.

All I can tell them is what I have told myself over the years, that none of us has the answers. Only God knows, or the Universe knows.

What I *do* know is that each time we face a challenge, we have five doors before us. It does not have to be five, per se. It could be three or it could be ten, but five is a good number. So, say we have a decision to make, and we decide there are five approaches to take.

Here is one approach: we can knock on the first door, and if it does not open, then we knock on the second and the third, and so on. This may take a while and we might build up a sense of rejection in our spirits so that, by the time we get to the fourth door, if it does not open, then we might lack the resolve or the will to knock on the fifth, so this strategy is no good.

Alternatively, we can pick a door at random, say the third door. But if we did not try the first two doors, we might be needlessly selecting a more difficult path for ourselves, and though we might never know it, we may have set ourselves back in time and resources which we could have used down the line to overcome another challenge. Therefore, this is not the best strategy either.

What is left? When the correct path is uncertain, this is what I tell people:

"If we have five doors before us, knock on all five at once."

Whichever door opens is the path that has been divined for us to take. No one has the luxury of waking up each morning and knowing whether to go left or go right, or to just walk straight and you will be fine. No. There is no such knowledge. We are all handicapped in not knowing what tomorrow will bring. What we do know is that today, we can knock at all five doors and one of them will be our pathway to a better tomorrow.

The same lessons in life and throughout history apply to the modern business landscape. Of course, anyone who has ever researched "starting a business" knows there are costs and risks associated with launching a new enterprise. One must assess the market, find and fill a void, or innovate something that exists and then find a way to bring it to market, maximize visibility, build a brand, and so forth. It can be incredibly difficult.

One example of someone who "got it right" is Reed Hastings, CEO and co-founder of Netflix. The story goes that in the late 1990s, VHS and DVD rental giant Blockbuster was king. But if a person lost or damaged a rental video, there were exorbitant fees to pay. Also, despite rows and rows of film options, inevitably, the one movie a person wanted to rent might be out on the night that they came. Plus, technology was rapidly advancing. There were drawbacks.

Hastings and his friend wondered if there was a way to serve the same niche but via mail, increasing the ease-of-use feature for the consumer by allowing them to shop on the web, select the film they wanted, and to receive and return it by mail. Simple enough. Hastings tested the idea by mailing himself a used CD through the U.S. Postal Service to validate that the concept was possible.

Needless to say, not only was the idea a success, it also set Netflix on the path to becoming the first streaming service to obtain global reach, ultimately rendering Blockbuster Video obsolete and launching the so-called streaming wars. All along the way, Hastings and co. had to find a way: find a way to do what Blockbuster did but better and find a way to improve on delivering movies and television shows into people's homes, entering new markets around the globe.

"For the first five years, it wasn't clear that we were going to survive," Hastings told CNBC in 2017.

And today, despite getting there first and having a head start, Netflix has a slew of competitors, including Apple T.V., Amazon Prime, Peacock (NBC), Hulu, Disney +, HBO Max, Paramount +, and more. Netflix has to continually find ways to improve its service to keep customers subscribed and entice new customers to tune in all the time. Despite being founded in 1997 and not making a profit until 2003, Netflix is now (Q3 2021) available to stream in more than 190 countries, offering original content in several of them as well as globally. It is also adopting successful social media best practices such as offering a Top 10 selection based on keeping track of data analytics that indicate the most-watched series, what is trending as well as what is new and what is to come in the next week or month.

In 2021, Netflix's worth increased to more than $260 billion. A business that started with a used CD and a stamp, which back then cost 32 cents, is now worth nearly $300 billion because a couple of friends opted to find a way to improve something that already existed. The company is the world's leading Internet television network, streaming in more than 190 countries.

They knocked on all possible doors to test and ultimately prove their idea could work.

This is why I say we must knock on all five doors. Netflix grew from a mail delivery service to a pioneering in-home streaming service because doors opened and closed for the company over time and as technology and consumer habits evolved, so too did the business model.

In my own life, I too have had to adapt over time. I had a set of goals that, to begin with, were not easily attained for anyone. Add to that my station in life as a boy, poor and in a relatively remote part of the world. I had to knock on many doors before one opened.

This continued when I came to the United States. When I settled in High Point, North Carolina, I decided I wanted to start my own practice, but no one would sell me theirs. I started by looking in the phone book and sending out letters to gauge interest from existing practices. I sent more than 100 letters in Greensboro, Winston-Salem, and in High Point. I got perhaps 10 responses in each setting, and no takers. Not until one man in High Point, Dr. N. Hampton Chiles, who was nearing his retirement agreed to meet me.

Suffice it to say he was not expecting a dark-skinned immigrant to walk into his office that day. Yet once we talked and he and I got to know each other, he saw something in me. He told me that if he did decide to sell his practice, he would only sell it to me, which he later did.

Soon after, once I began to see some success within my own practice, it became clear to me that running a specialty practice such as gastroenterology made me dependent on other physicians referring patients my way. Additionally, as the cost of health care and medical insurance began to rise, as did malpractice insurance for doctors, hospitals began to swallow up independent practices. It was easier for doctors to align with the larger health systems and reduce their costs to stay afloat. I knew I did not want to close up shop, but I also knew I did not want to work for anyone else. I needed to find a way.

Then, a lightning bolt of an idea struck me: open a multi-specialty practice. If I were going to need patient referrals to operate as a gastroenterologist, why not start a primary care practice where patients would come to my clinic for all types of ailments? I could treat them as well as hire other doctors, physician's assistants, and nurse practitioners who could also see patients. And when a patient needed specialist care, I could refer them. Rather than send them across town to someone else, though, I would refer them down the hall to myself or another doctor in my employ.

I started Bethany Medical Center with the idea that I would not turn away a person in need of care, and we do not. We are open seven days a week, we take care of everyone who comes through our doors regardless of their ability to pay, and we sort out the details after. Other doctors thought I was crazy and were certain I would fail.

I knew better.

And yet, I hit a major roadblock. Sure, today Bethany Medical and its 15 locations across the Piedmont Triad treat more than 1,100 patients per day. But only because I found a way. When I was denied a loan to buy the building into which I wanted to move my practice, I went around the bank to the owner directly and negotiated a price. I found a way.

When I wanted to expand my practice to include multi-specialty care, I hired other specialists and nurses. I wanted a diverse staff to demonstrate to the community that people of all colors and backgrounds could work together and deliver the same care as or better than an all-white practice. And we did so. I found a way.

Today, I am the largest independent single-owner medical care provider in North Carolina because I found a way.

Yes, I had butterflies in my stomach at times. Yes, I wondered early if taking on debt to buy another physician's practice was a good idea. Yes, I was rejected for a loan and denied the purchase of a building and, yes, I ran into obstacles because of the color of my skin and the accent with which I speak. But I found a way.

Each time I was denied entry through the front door, I tried a side door. And if I were denied entry through the side door, I tried the back door. You can, too. The only person who can tell you that you cannot do something and be 100 percent accurate when they say it is you.

"It always seems impossible until it's done."

NELSON MANDELA

PRINCIPLE #3 TAKEAWAYS

- There is always a back or side door that will solve your challenge.
- Filter out your deep-seated rationalizations for "why it cannot be done."
- Channel your inner Mark Cuban, who famously said, "work like there is someone working 24 hours a day to take it all away from you."

SECTION II
DAILY AFFIRMATIONS

"I remind myself each morning: Nothing I say this day
will teach me anything. So, if I am going to learn, I must
do it by listening."

LARRY KING

PRINCIPLE #4:

LISTEN AND LEARN

"The art of conversation lies in listening."
MALCOLM FORBES

When I tell people that I manage my own stock portfolio, very often they laugh at me. But that is my approach, without an advisor or a professional to manage my holdings. This may surprise them, but that is not the funny part. No, their laughter usually comes after I tell them how I do so. I admit, I laugh as well.

First though, understand that I have limited time to divert outside of my work. Work is fun for me, and I am happiest and most excited when at work. I do not need "work-life balance," because my life is well balanced at work.

I tend to keep busy, even at this stage in my life. But then, I always have kept busy. Running seven companies with more than 600 employees and keeping tabs on my interests in banking and commercial real estate development, as well as operating the multi-site, multi-specialty clinic Bethany Medical, constitutes a lifetime job rather than a full-time position. I have edged away from the day-to-day operations now ably run by my daughter, Elise Peters Carey. Although I do advise her, I also continue to have many responsibilities that necessitate my attention. My days are consumed.

One respite I have comes when I travel, which I do often, particularly between my three main hubs of operation, High Point, North Carolina; Manhattan, New York; and Miami Beach, Florida. I tend to either continue working or catch up on rest while in the air, but one of my favorite things to do happens after landing.

I turn on my internal antennae, my ears, which are finely tuned to pick up critical information.

I like to travel from the airport to whatever my destination might be, the hotel, a board meeting, etc., by taxi. Today, rideshare companies seem to be the preferred means of hiring a car, but I still enjoy taxis. It is from the backseat of the humble, old-school taxi that I often gain some of the most fruitful insight into world affairs and the stock market. And here is where most people laugh. And I do as well. Yes, I get some of my best investment advice from taxi drivers.

While this is no slight to the profession or the professionals who drive taxis, this is not a job in which one would expect the person to have great insight or working knowledge of the markets, where inflation is, or what the Federal Reserve is up to. One individual driver may possess more knowledge or insight than others, but for the most part, this is not an expectation of the job.

Still, I like to ask the driver how he sees the economy or if he knows what the stock markets are up to. If, for instance, the driver tells me he just purchased some stocks or that he feels the stock market is doing well, I learn by listening to him that the information he has used to make his investment decisions has worked its way from the respective publicly traded companies through the brokerage firms and hedge funds up and down Wall Street and into the mainstream, down through the finance publications and television news networks' business segments to the average citizen. If the cab driver knows the market is up, this tells me what other, more savvy investors are likely thinking in real time. It is too late to buy.

I consider selling a portion of my portfolio and taking what profits I've made.

If, instead, the driver tells me that the market has turned, the economy stinks, and everyone is losing money, this too is valuable information. If the average investor has the sense that the market is bad and everyone is taking losses, this means that prices are low, and it is the right time for me to invest.

I go and buy.

Using this strategy and others, I have always been able to outperform the stock market by an average of 30 to 50 percent. Don't get me wrong; this is not the only piece of information I use. I do my own research and evaluate the stock market in many other ways, but this is one tool I continue to use. My internal antenna pulls in even the weakest signal.

This is a small example of the power of listening. Every bit of what someone tells you informs you of something. Now, if you have reason not to trust the person based on something you know about them, you might know there is a chance their information is bad or that they are lying to you. But even if this is the case, you might discern from what they choose to tell you what their true intentions are. Maybe you know something has been omitted and so by assessing what they said and did not say, you can glean what piece of information they intended to keep from you and perhaps why.

If you do trust the person and you are not listening to them to learn what they know, you might listen instead to learn how they think or why they believe what they do. If you are in business with or doing business with someone and they often mention their religion or political views or their family or sailing or cats and dogs and horses and sheep, whatever it may be, you now know their passion.

Leaders who know how to listen can maximize their team's productivity and morale. Why? Because such leaders learn, by listening, what motivates and inspires people—the organization's most prized asset. Understand your people's goals, dreams, and aspirations, and you are positioned for success.

Leaders who listen go into negotiations with an edge. They know where the other person's genuine interests are and where they will—or won't—be flexible. When you are on a board or committee and you hope to sway the other members to vote the way you hope they will on an upcoming agenda item, you will know how to speak to them and gain their confidence. Or vice versa. If someone is trying to sway your opinion or influence you to join their side, by listening skillfully, you might discern whether they truly believe their way is the best to achieve the intended goal or if perhaps they have a dog in the fight and are seeking some individual gain that does not serve the interest of the company or community.

The fact is we listen all day long to everyone and everything, but we do not always process what we hear or give credence to what we are being told. Our internal antennae are highly directional. Sometimes we must turn our antennae this way and that to maximize "reception," much like the analog radios of old.

Skillful listening requires that we actively engage in what we are hearing or being told and focus and give full attention to the person speaking. Relationships are forged and fractured, deals are consummated and broken, opportunities are seized and missed, and businesses are built and dissolved based on whether or not we actively and skillfully listen.

And, as with the taxi driver example, it is not always the most highly educated or experienced person from whom the best information or brightest idea will arise. Companies spend millions on focus groups and test marketing, and nowadays data mining programs, to gain insight into what consumers are thinking. Knowing what drives people to buy a product or pay for a service is greatly important, as is knowing when they are most likely to buy, and at what price.

The advance of micro-targeting consumer groups is an example of digital "listening." Companies assess consumer habits down to the zip code and learn which branch of which store people in a given community frequent, as well as what they purchase, at what price, and at what time of day.

Say CVS Pharmacy is rolling out a new healthcare program tailored to Hispanic people over 65. There will be more marketing materials, digital ads, signage, mailers, and promotional flyers distributed in zip codes of major cities across the country with denser populations of older Hispanic men and women. CVS locations on sides of town with more sizeable White or African American populations would see different messaging.

In relationships, too, we often learn from our interactions with those around us how best to communicate and interact with one another. A misunderstanding with our significant other, for instance, may result in a disagreement. When things calm down, we might learn that our partner told us something not so we would act but so that we would understand their position or their thought process and feelings. We missed an opportunity to empathize because we were *hearing* rather than listening.

We can cause our loved ones great pain, and we can introduce strain on our relationships needlessly if we do not listen and seek to understand what we are being told. The same is true in business and in politics and wherever else the stakes are high, and where ideas and opinions vary widely.

Great world leaders have risen to power because they listened to their people. Conversely, sometimes leaders fall from greatness because they do not listen to the people or to their trusted advisors.

Former leader of the U.S.S.R. Mikhail Gorbachev is both hailed and criticized for his role in the fall of the Soviet bloc. He ascended to power after several short-lived tenures of his predecessors, mostly older men who died not long after taking control. And his tenure came on the heels of several decades of oppression and internal strife under such men as Joseph Stalin and Nikita Khrushchev. The period between the end of World War II and the fall of the U.S.S.R. saw much of Eastern Europe swallowed up by the communist Russian regime, splitting the continent into East and West. The wall represented the separation of the democratic West and the communist East, which fell quietly under a blanket of oppression and isolation, cut off from the rest of the world.

Revisionist history today tells us that U.S. President Ronald Reagan is credited with ending the Cold War and toppling the Kremlin with his 1987 speech in Berlin, during which he uttered the now-famous phrase, "Mr. Gorbachev, tear down this wall." The reference was to the Berlin Wall, erected 26 years earlier and which divided the capital city of Berlin, Germany, into East Germany and West Germany. The wall and capital city halved at its middle had long since become the physical manifestation of the Cold War, the epitome of the global battle for dominance between democracy and communism, with the U.S. and Western Europe on one side, and Russia and China on the other.

While Reagan's words were powerful, and in hindsight, did coincide with the beginning of the end—the Berlin Wall fell two years later—of the U.S.S.R., Gorbachev was already years into his agenda and policymaking that sought to turn the communist republic into a more democratic, capitalist society. Americans 40 or older today might recall the terms *Glasnost* and *Perestroika*, Russian terms for "opening" and "restructuring."

Looking back, Gorbachev might have moved too quickly. For a widespread nation as vast as Russia to reform in a matter of years is akin to an aircraft carrier making a three-point turn in the middle of the ocean. It is a rather difficult undertaking sure to cause discomfort in the process.

And did it.

The U.S.S.R. economy was already destabilized, and Eastern European nations once under the thumb of the communist regime began to reclaim independence and hold democratic elections.

Gorbachev, whose reforms sought to give more protection to personal freedoms and freedom of the press in Russia, fell victim to his own policies and the economic and civil turmoil that unfolded.

A weak and corrupt government succeeded Gorbachev's Russia. Once America's greatest rival in the space race and nuclear arms acceleration and the world's second-largest economy behind only the U.S., Russia's world position eroded.

So, what does all of this have to do with listening? First, Gorbachev listened to his people. He saw that the oppressive state propped up by tyrannical rule and enforced through violence, murder, and reprisal was untenable. He knew that sustained posturing with the U.S. in the arms and space races would sooner or later culminate in disaster for all. And he listened to Reagan throughout a series of ongoing talks held in neutral locations such as Reykjavik, Iceland. While he later dismissed Reagan's speech, saying he and his administration knew the U.S. president's first career had been as an actor, the private meetings with Reagan demonstrated to Gorbachev there was an opportunity to enact his reforms and stave off a third world war in the process.

This story's second lesson on listening comes from Reagan's side. His speech at the time was not well received. Many in the U.S. State Department and the National Security Council deemed the speech too aggressive for the moment and feared it would further chill relations between the two global powers. But Reagan, hearing his advisors out, weighed the arguments for and against leaving the line in. The speech's author, Peter Robinson,[6] recounted in a 2007 article that the debate raged on right up until the president was in the limousine on the way to deliver the officially dubbed Brandenburg Gate Address. This is an example of the president actively listening right up until the last possible moment.

Reagan was determined to deliver the line, Robinson writes. He goes on to quote the president as saying why.

"The boys at State are going to kill me, but it's the right thing to do," Robinson quoted Reagan.

At the time, Reagan's words were considered both controversial and less intimidating than some would have preferred. But they do reverberate through time. In retrospect, it was the right message delivered in the right place at the right time. Both the speechwriter and president used their listening skills to their best advantage, and knew it would impact the people who mattered, those who lived on either side of the wall.

Within two years the wall would come down, and the U.S.S.R. would implode, ushering a new set of circumstances into the final decade of a

6 "'Tear Down This Wall:' How Top Advisors Opposed Reagan's Challenge to Gorbachev, But Lost." Peter Robinson, 2007, Vo. 39. No. 2, U.S. National Archives, archives.gov.

century that had seen two world wars, the Cold War, and the rise of two global superpowers, only one of which was left standing at the end.

The 1990s saw the birth of something else as well. The Internet both connected the world and brought about a tech boom—later recast as the dot-com bubble—which saw the quick rise of a mass of new companies and then the devastating fall of the U.S. stock market when the so-called bubble finally burst.

More devastating, though, and more pertinent to this very chapter would be the next major economic crisis to plague the U.S., the greatest collapse since the Great Depression, now known as the Great Recession. The housing bubble, created by and then paid for dearly by banks and financial institutions that were trading bundled mortgages, made fortunes for investors. Called subprime mortgages, these exorbitant loans put people into homes much larger than they could afford and saw many people living the high life for a while. And then, all at once, it came crashing down.

I saw early on that this was taking place, and I knew not only was it risky, but it was also immoral. To offer people loans banks knew they could not afford to pay back was to set people up to fail intentionally. Foreclosures skyrocketed along with the investment portfolios of these greedy bankers and hedge fund managers, and it was not long before entire neighborhoods of homes purchased with these subprime mortgages were foreclosed and sitting empty.

The banks that initiated these loans bundled them together by the hundreds and sold them off to larger institutions for a substantial profit. The larger institutions bundled these packaged mortgages with other packages now in the thousands and sold them off to investment firms and international banks. Synthetics, the "engineered wood" of financial instruments.

The eventual outcome was inevitable, and everyone involved seemed to know it. The only thing no one knew for sure was the right time to get out, to sell off what remaining mortgage bundles a firm or investor owned before anyone came to cash in.

Things got so bad that often no one knew who held the deed for a particular home and lawsuits began to emerge between people living in foreclosed homes and the banks looking to repossess the dwelling. Neither legally held the deed which had been bought and sold and re-bundled and bought and sold again several times over.

At that time, I was the chairman of the loan committee for the Bank of North Carolina, and a founding member of the bank. I told our management and our board we would not engage in such practices. I was adamant about it, and I did not care how much money other institutions were making. We would continue to offer traditional loans to applicants who were vetted and qualified to receive them and who could most certainly pay them back. Most borrowers did, in fact, do just that.

BNC grew to become BNC Bank Corp., operating in three states. Ultimately the bank was sold to Pinnacle Financial Partners and continued to do very well, due in large measure to its avoidance of the subprime mortgage game.

In hindsight, we made the right decision. I listened to the people who were for it, and I heard their arguments that there was a lot of money to be made very quickly and easily. I also listened to our clients who, when they came to us for a loan, told us what their financial situation was and what they could afford to borrow and pay back.

I did not have to weigh the two options for long. Despite being immoral and a rotten thing to do, these were our neighbors. If we loaned them money to buy real estate they could not afford, we would ultimately have to repossess the property and evict the residents or small business owners. We would eventually be putting our own clients out of business and depleting the tax base of our own city. I am glad we listened to our clients as well as our conscience and did not engage in this activity. Unfortunately, so many other banks jumped into this market.

Entire industries were wiped out in the 2008 collapse. Those companies that had not already farmed out most of their operations to Asia and to Central and South America either did so after the economy crashed, or they simply went out of business. The effects were devastating for the nation and for our own community.

Only now, nearly 15 years later, is our local economy re-emerging through investment in new companies, entrepreneurial efforts, and a revitalization effort led by a group of developers, including myself, who share a vision of a livable downtown in our community of High Point.

In recent years, we've faced a new challenge that required nuanced calibration of our internal antennae. The pandemic has taken a toll, with more economic difficulty heaped on small business owners. But again, by listening to the community and hearing what people want and need, in a community where folks can live where they work, we are rebuilding what the Great Recession and Covid-19 pandemic helped to erase.

> **"We have two ears and one tongue
> so that we would listen more and talk less."**
> DIOGENES

PRINCIPLE #4 TAKEAWAYS

- A great advantage to superior listeners is this human trait: people LOVE to talk.

- Listen hard to the thoughts of those from all walks of life, not just from your immediate circle (the dreaded, so-called "echo chamber").

- The bigger the challenge, the greater the obstacle, the more intently you need to listen

PRINCIPLE #5:

THINK BIG

"Belief triggers the power to do."
– DAVID JOSEPH SCHWARTZ

There is a quote from self-help author Norman Vincent Peale that I often point to when trying to inspire others to think beyond their stated goals or aspirations. In his bestseller *The Power of Positive Thinking*,[7] Peale suggests that we should "Shoot for the moon. Even if you miss, you'll land among the stars."

The message is simple and a key to your success. Imagine the greatest accomplishment you can dream of, and work toward that goal. Even if you fall a bit short, you will still have achieved so much more than you would have chasing a smaller and more attainable goal.

---

7 *The Power of Positive Thinking.* Norman Vincent Peale. Prentice Hall, U.S.; 1952.

I distill this message into two words: Think Big! We are only limited by our ability to dream. In addition, we all have different drivers and dream of different things. For example, not everyone seeks to be the richest person in the world or the one with the most material assets. Nor does every employee set his or her sights on becoming the CEO. Not all of us hope to one day become the most famous movie star, our name in the lights above the marquee. A person might aspire to be the best team member they can be to inspire others, or to help 100 people in their community in some way over the next year. Others may strive to become the first person in their family to earn a college degree.

Thinking big applies to material rewards, as well as to personal, inner accomplishments. Self-esteem and respect for oneself help foster integrity and honesty, attributes that are demanded of anyone who seeks to become or to remain successful and a good citizen of the world.

So far in this book we have learned to do things right away, to act quickly while the opportunity exists. We have adopted the discipline to stop lying to ourselves and being our own worst enemies. We have learned what it means to truly listen, and we are employing that practice now, too. And when obstacles are placed in our path, we are encouraged to stay determined and find a way.

Thinking big, the next rung in our ladder to success, demands that we apply all of what we have learned so far in this book, and that we stretch our imaginations like rubber bands to conceive more for ourselves, our businesses, our families, and communities.

However, it is my real hope that you are beginning to realize that inner drive, discipline, and morality are not mutually exclusive. Think of them as the three legs of a stool. Take away one leg, and the stool will wobble. Each element is essential to success.

And the more we succeed, the more we come to trust, develop, and apply our good habits, healthy practices, and sound strategies. The more we *share* our success by helping those around us, teaching others what we have learned, and being someone who opens a door when someone else knocks, be it a side door or a back door, then the more we can say we have truly succeeded.

Thinking big brought me first to the U.K. from India, then from the U.K. to the U.S. I wanted to be a doctor to heal people and improve life for those around me. Yet I also wanted to ensure financial security for my family back home, my own growing family, and my future grandchildren and great-grandchildren.

When I came to the South, to High Point, North Carolina, I wanted to be my own boss and so I found a way to buy another doctor's practice and begin my own business. I then saw where the health care industry was heading, and I wanted to secure my own future and that of my patients. I set out to build a self-sustaining, multi-specialty practice that could grow while caring for every patient that came through its doors. And we have done that.

I learned along my journey that investing in real estate provided a means to build wealth for my family. I created a portfolio of rental properties, first residential and then commercial, and used this new knowledge and wealth to grow my medical practice to 15 locations, to construct office buildings and now mixed-use retail, commercial, and residential buildings that will help revitalize downtown High Point and benefit our community for generations to follow.

Another example: my team and I saw a need for business banking access in our own community, and we built it from the ground up. We then saw that our model was successful and so we grew it to the point we expanded into three states and ultimately merged with a regional bank.

In each of these examples, any of which could stand alone and be considered a success in its own right, I started with a primary goal, and I thought big in expanding it. One success led to another, leading to more financial gain for my family as well as for our community. The cycle of thinking big continues.

There are many ways to give back, or "pay it forward." I wanted to do more than write checks to charities and donate sums at fundraisers, although these are important endeavors that I still do today. However, I felt there was more that we could do to positively impact the world immediately and for the foreseeable future.

I decided to start the Lenny Peters Foundation, and when I did, I don't mind saying, many people laughed and said I was being impractical. As you know by now, this was not the first instance others laughed at one of my big ideas. I smiled and knew I would make them see just how right I was.

When someone attaches his or her name to something, be it a building or a foundation or a recurring event, some will point out and say it was done for ego. This is not untrue, for there is pride attached to undertaking such a large effort and in having reached a point in one's life where the means are available to fund it.

Yet this is far from the root of the tree or the primary motivation that sustains the effort. If that were the case, I could have opened the Lenny Peters Car Wash and Drive-in Movie Emporium and splashed my name across the nation with franchise locations in every major city. This is a silly example to make a point. But this was not about self-aggrandizement. This was something different. I wanted to build something that would last beyond my own life, that would continue to provide for people and create possibilities for those who had limited advantages.

I am happy to say that we have been able to do just that, not only here in the U.S. or in my native India, but worldwide.

Today the Lenny Peters Foundation, in addition to its local causes and campaigns, fully funds activities and nine centers on three continents—Asia, Africa, and North America. We are truly an international foundation, running several orphanages and homes for the poor and terminally ill. These include in India, the Jayamatha Boys Home; the Lenny Peters Home for Girls; the Lenny Peters Home for Palliative Care ; the Lenny Peters Prayer Center; the Lenny Peters Girls Home; the Lenny Peters Divine Mercy Home; and the Lenny Peters Home for the Elderly, and in South Africa, the Lenny Peters Home for Children and the Lenny Peters Welfare Center for Children .

More information about these respective centers as well as images and videos can be found on the Foundation website, LennyPetersFoundation.org.

The first three centers are, as their respective names imply, one orphanage each for boys and for girls in India, as well as a home for the sick and dying. The Lenny Peters Prayer Center is a nunnery where the ordained sisters pray 24 hours each day, both their own prayers and those requested by others to be prayed on their behalf.

At the Lenny Peters Girls Home , we take young girls who have been or would be targeted by human trafficking and protect them from being sold into slavery. And finally, the Lenny Peters Home for Children is now operating in Johannesburg, South Africa, with the blessing of the local Archbishop.

The Lenny Peters Divine Mercy Home is a worship center for the regional community in southern India, and the Lenny Peters Welfare Center is where poor children are educated and cared for throughout the day in the northern part of South India.

We are still growing, and I am encouraged by our success so far. My faith is also strengthened to see that I, along with so many others who have sacrificed their time and energy to help us along the way, have been able to help so many people. We now serve up to 300 people per day, in addition to those at our nine centers, who are in need of help in poor villages. I am reminded of Mother Teresa, canonized in 2016 as a Catholic saint for her lifetime of charitable works. She spent her entire life, from a teenager until her death at 87, serving the poorest of the poor and the sickest of the sick.

It is my hope that in the same way, through the Lenny Peters Foundation, we can care for and protect the children and the sick who are still living and to cater to the ill and dying in their last days so that they know someone cares for them before they leave this world.

Mother Teresa started a home for lepers in India when no one wanted to help or even see or touch these afflicted people. She turned that first center into many and then included hospices and orphanages as well. By her death in 1997, Mother Teresa had established 517 missions in 100 countries. Today, the Lenny Peters Foundation has nine centers, and although it will require much more dedication and hard work, and support from our friends, 500 centers is not out of our reach. Not if we think big!

History favors wisdom that anticipates the needs of the times. We revere the champions of impossible causes, even though in their own lifetimes, they were mocked or ignored. When a challenge is great enough, a reward so promising, or a competitor so bent on an accomplishment, man somehow finds a way to dig deep and tackle what until that very moment has been deemed impossible. This is only accomplished by those who think big.

President John F. Kennedy, as a speaker, may most famously be remembered for this line in his inaugural address, "Ask not what your country can do for you—ask what you can do for your country."

This profound reminder that the United States is not only a nation of its people and for its people, but one built *by* its people, reinvigorated a nation on the verge of being torn apart by war and social unrest. The next decade would test this idea in ways Kennedy himself could not have imagined. Still, it was another line in a later speech where Kennedy instilled in the masses the idea to think big.

Kennedy addressed a sea of dignitaries as well as scientists and engineers on the campus of Rice University in Houston, Texas, on September 12, 1962. A new decade was underway, and with it, the race to space. Remember that Russia had developed an aggressive space program.

Back then, Houston, now synonymous with NASA, was the epicenter of the U.S.' nascent effort to explore the final frontier: outer space. Naysayers considered the very notion too difficult and far too costly. Kennedy knew he needed public support to push the initiative to the forefront and inspire the nation to do something that as of yet had existed only in the imagination of science fiction writers.

In what would come to be known as the "Moon Speech," Kennedy made the impossible seem plausible and not only that, but he also linked the effort to American exceptionalism. Success, should Americans achieve it, could be worn as a badge of pride for decades to come.

"We choose to go to the moon," Kennedy said. "We choose to go to the moon in this decade and do the other things not because they are easy but because they are hard…."

Fourteen months later, in the same state of Texas, President Kennedy would be killed by an assassin's bullet. His vision of American preeminence in space, however, would live on and come to fruition within the decade. On July 20, 1969, American men landed on the moon and later safely returned to Earth.

So much of the technology consumers now rely on and so gladly pay for was first made possible by the efforts of the men and women who made space travel and satellites and telecommunications real, tangible, and functional. Big ideas that required the most minute detail and precision to achieve are now everyday household items.

What will exist tomorrow or 10 years from now or 100 years from now because you, or your company, or your children were inspired to think big?

Elon Musk and his company SpaceX are but one of the private sector companies that may someday bring man safely to Mars. Judging by the drive of these visionaries, future success seems inevitable. Man will continue to reach into space and seek to explore and conquer new frontiers. What is mankind but a series of generations who take up the mantle of those who have gone before, see what exists and what needs to be done, make improvements, imagine what could be, and then create it?

Being an entrepreneur then is a very human endeavor, is it not? The same drive is required to solve problems and make life easier, make devices and processes more efficient and cost effective, and make products more sustainable to reduce waste and pollution and to preserve the environment.

Some efforts succeed, and others fail. Often, the only difference between those who last and grow and those who struggle and barely survive is the ability to keep thinking big—even in the face of overwhelming odds.

Steve Jobs is known as the man behind the success of Apple Inc. Originally a co-founder of the company that helped introduce personal computers to the world in the '70s, Jobs was later forced out of the company. He would go on to start his own computer development company and grow it to huge success.

Jobs helped direct the company that developed into Disney's Pixar Animation Studios, the producers of such films as the "Toy Story" franchise and many more. And, of course, later Jobs would return to the company he helped found and steer Apple from near bankruptcy to unprecedented success with the advent of technologies now taken for granted such as the iPhone, iTunes, and iPad, to name a few.

Jobs is a prime example of a person who thought big throughout his entire, albeit all too short, lifetime. Jobs died of cancer in 2011, at the age of 56, but not before he helped to create so much of what we see and use throughout our daily lives. Of course, there are probably tens of thousands of engineers and developers and programmers who might never get the credit for their individual contributions, but Jobs led the companies that are credited with these inventions and innovations. He did not just show up at the end of the day to hold the microphone and bask in the applause.

It takes untold vision to lead a company from the brink of collapse to the top of the stock market. As this is written , Apple is trading at more than $160 per share. Fourteen years ago, it was trading at about $6 per share. Not a bad return.

It takes a person who not only sees and thinks of grand ideas but who can inspire others to do the same and who can steer a company through financial difficulty, over political potholes, and around social roadblocks to succeed. In the 1990s, Bill Gates and Microsoft dominated the computerized world. By the time of Jobs' death, there was either an iPod, iPhone, or iPad in nearly every home in the country. Today, the company competes in the smartphone and personal computer spaces, music and television streaming service industries, film and animation, and the vast expanse that is the world of apps.

What one can accomplish is truly only limited by the extent to which one is willing to think big and work hard. The same is true in charitable works and in business as well as in leading a nation. There is a saying (attributed by some to Friedrich Wilhelm Nietzsche, the German philosopher and poet) that the "devil is in the details." Yes, I do not wish to mislead anyone by saying thinking big *always* leads to success. There will be failure, there will be setbacks, and there will be insurmountable obstacles. It is precisely in those moments when we are tested and tired that we must conjure up the energy and the will to think big, overcome, and persevere.

We must always work hard, pay attention to the details, and surround ourselves with people who are as committed to doing so as we are, who are great at what they do and can be entrusted to do their part as we are asking them to trust us to do ours. Mother Teresa received the Nobel Peace Prize, the Presidential Medal of Freedom, the Congressional Gold Medal, and the Albert Schweitzer International Prize, among countless other awards and honors. Still, she remained committed to her work in helping people and any monetary prize she was awarded she put solely into that effort. She entered the world a poor girl from Skopje and left it as a world figure, granted sainthood some years after her death.

President Kennedy was the son of a bootlegger who went on to first become a war hero after being wounded in World War II while serving in the U.S. Navy and later became President of the United States. Steve Jobs dropped out of college and was forced out of the company he would later return to not only run, but rescue. Today, his name is synonymous with that company and its pervasive products.

While I do not assume to place myself on the same rung with any of these figures, I too came from very humble beginnings. I worked my way through life's obstacles, taking calculated chances to succeed. I can now leave a legacy for my family and the many communities I serve. What I share in common with these historical figures (and, hopefully, you will as well) is our ability to think big and go out and *do*.

Who knows, by shooting for the moon today, you might one day, many years from now, find yourself standing among the stars.

> **"If people aren't calling you crazy, you aren't thinking big enough."**
> RICHARD BRANSON

PRINCIPLE #5 TAKEAWAYS

- The foundation of success includes the ability to Think Big.
- Stretch your imagination to envision accomplishments that benefit you and your world.
- Make no mistake: it takes guts to think big, especially in the face of societal disparagement.
- Ask yourself: Why not shoot for the moon?

PRINCIPLE #6:

COMMIT

"Commitment is what transforms
a promise into a reality."
ABRAHAM LINCOLN

Here you are. You have come up with the big idea that, unlike the others before, is guaranteed to take hold. Thinking big has brought you this far, and you have listened to your team and stopped lying to yourself. You are ready for success. All that is left is to go out and do it.

"So, now what?" you ask yourself.

Some may laugh, but others will identify immediately with that moment of hesitation. All the planning and preparation in the world is for naught if the strategy devised is never implemented. Fear or lack of discipline can derail the best-laid plans right out of the gate if one is not mentally ready to work, lead, and commit.

The term "commit" can be used to convey different meanings. Whereas one might commit an act, one might also commit themselves to an idea, a purpose, a cause.

The way I see it, to *commit* is to pledge. Commitment connotes dedication to a sense of honor. Duty. It is a vow. A sacred vow.

One must commit with fierce dedication to one's own success. No one else will do it for you. Not your team, not your bank or financiers, not even your spouse or children will believe in your big idea if you do not unfailingly demonstrate your own belief and dedication. And I do mean unfailingly.

I have recounted in earlier chapters instances where I took great risks, made promises to myself, and found alternative means when I was denied traditional pathways to accomplish my own goals. I am proud to say I had help along the way, surrounded by great team members and dedicated people who saw my vision and were inspired to come along and contribute to the same cause. They were able to do so readily and willingly because they saw my commitment and no hint of surrender or defeat in my eyes, even when times were difficult, or things did not go as planned.

This is not by accident. For me, failure was simply not an option. There was no instance in which I would accept defeat. I would not be denied or rejected because of my immigrant status, dark skin or thick accent, faith, or lack of finances or experience. The prejudices I encountered were not mine to overcome but, rather, those of the people who harbored them. My only duty? To forgive them for their ignorance and move forward, with or without them. I knew in my heart that I would acquire financial strength and business acumen over time with hard work and further education.

Believe it or not, when I first started my medical practice, I had never run a business before, so I had a lot to learn. I knew nothing about billing and receivables, labor laws, and employee management. Still, my big idea was to own a practice and then use that as a launchpad for bigger things.

The other factor I alluded to was money—I had none. Yes, I was a doctor and had some small real estate investments, but I had also spent a great deal of money relocating, getting married, and starting a family. I had an 18-month-old baby, and my wife was six months pregnant. I had been in training for many years, repeating my residency as required every time I moved to a new country (four continents in all). This meant that although I had been a doctor for many years, seeing patients and gaining experience, I had never been fully employed.

Most doctors, or about 90 percent of them, do not go the route I chose. More often a doctor coming out of training negotiates a salary and lands a job. It is a steady paycheck, with a bonus, a retirement plan, vacation, and various benefits.

That is the norm. I am not putting them down, but that is normally the way it goes. And, of course, they will be making $300,000 or $400,000 or $500,000 a year. I chose to start my own practice, so rather than a guaranteed salary with a slate of incentives, I would instead be taking on debt. I did not realize at first just how much debt I would be facing.

I negotiated the purchase of my first practice from its original owner, Dr. N. Hampton Chiles, who was an amazing southern gentleman. He trained at the Mayo Clinic, had been in practice for 25 years, had all the best patients and staff, and was beloved by his community. It was a miracle that he was persuaded to sell the practice to me. Not only that, but he said if he were going to sell to anyone, he would only sell to me. This was an honor. And I took on the challenge.

But he was tough.

He said, "I can take you to the water, Lenny, but you still have to drink it."

I remember this very clearly. Thus was my commitment.

I said, "I will drink that water. You take me there."

The price he negotiated was very steep. He asked for $250,000 up front and then he would stay on for at least two years at $120,000 per year. He would work for me, but on day one, I would be the boss. Upon agreeing to these terms, I instantly found myself $490,000 in debt. This was 35 years ago, in 1987. Even then, half a million dollars was a deep hole for a young doctor on day one of owning his own practice.

Now, for contrast, had I invested that money in the stock market rather than in my business, say in a Dow Jones index fund which has increased seven-fold over the last 35 years, my return would have been more than $3.4 million. For the average person, a 35-year window to realize a nest egg of close to $3.5 million dollars would have been a sound investment strategy for retirement.

Yet if I had done so, I would not be anywhere near where I am today. Nor would I have been able to help so many people along the way, both through the building of my various companies and all the people we have employed over the years, and through the 15 locations at Bethany Medical. These things all came to fruition as I envisioned, and so, for me, the risk was worth taking.

I took on the debt and set to work realizing my vision every step of the way. That was the commitment. That is how you get somewhere. I committed my time, my energy, all the years of training and what little money I had. I gave everything I had; all I could spare. And it was successful. With those things in mind and with my faith in God and the angels He continued to place in my path—the people along my journey whom I encountered, befriended, and who joined my team—how could I fail?

I could not. Neither will you, if you muster that degree of commitment, which I equate to that of a racehorse. A racehorse is fitted with blinders over its eyes, allowing it to see straight ahead and preventing the animal from being spooked by distractions in the periphery. Neither the roar of the crowd nor the other horses running alongside the gallant beast will deter it from going forward, running with abandon, with only the jockey to prod and position it.

This is the tunnel vision, the single-mindedness, needed throughout the entire process to achieve success. We must be mindful that distractions will always exist. It is our responsibility to filter them, or at least not be hindered by them.

As you have come to understand by this point in the book, I am fascinated by history and historical figures who met great challenges in their times. I can now think of no greater challenge, or one that would have required greater commitment, than that of George Washington, tapped to lead the Continental Army against the undefeated British Army in close-quarters engagement on the open battlefield.

The emerging nation had no standing Army at the time, only militias formed by and with allegiances to each individual colony. The Continental Congress held little money for supplies or uniforms and throughout much of the war, Washington's men had to do without proper clothing, weapons and ammunition, or food and supplies. History books are filled with accounts of requests by the General, many penned in his own hand, pleading with Congress for the necessities his men required to wage the war for American independence.

Despite being ill-equipped, Washington and his army fought on. Early in the war, when he found himself outmanned and outmaneuvered, Washington escaped with entire regiments of men from Long Island, and then Manhattan, ceding the vital port of New York to the British. This defeat and others like it threatened to crush American resolve.

Indeed, Washington was losing the confidence of his men and that of the Congress. He never faltered, however, in his commitment to the cause, and through a network of spies and intelligence gathering, the General was able to harass and harangue the enemy using unconventional military strategies. Today we might call some of these tactics guerilla warfare. That is, surprise assaults and brief skirmishes meant to inflict casualties and keep the enemy guessing rather than clash on open battlefields until attrition determines a victor.

There are numerous examples of this highlighted by historians who put together accounts held in private diaries and letters written by some of those engaged in Washington's secret intelligence networks[8]. Accounts reveal such daring missions as getting information into and out of New York and Boston, then British strongholds, where sympathetic citizens acted as covert agents to inform the colonies' cause. More commonly known, if not idealistically depicted in art and film, was the bold crossing of the icy Delaware River in the dead of night on Christmas Day in 1776[9]. Washington led an assault by boat across the river on a garrison of German mercenaries known as the Hessians, who were fighting on behalf of the British.

Catching them unaware, Washington and company overtook the Hessians with ease, gaining supplies and a temporary geographical advantage over the nearby British forces. This great raid is credited by historians with bolstering morale and patriot support for the war by demonstrating the Continental Army's ability to secure a victory in battle.

---

8 *Washington's Spies: The Story of America's First Spy Ring*. Alexander Rose; Bantam, April 2006.
9 *Washington's Crossing*. David Hackett Fischer; Oxford University Press, 2004.

The following winter at Valley Forge, 20 miles north of British-occupied Philadelphia, Washington defended himself from an intended coup by his detractors while pleading with the Continental Congress for support on behalf of his freezing men, who, without food or proper winter gear, were on the brink of starvation in frigid winter weather. Historians credit the General's leadership and the loyalty of his junior officers with getting the beleaguered Army through the winter and readying the forces to resume the fight come spring[10].

Although much more had to happen to overtake the occupying forces, including long-awaited assistance from the French, Washington managed to stay the course, his blinders on, and remain steadfast in the face of certain defeat to eventually emerge victorious.

Months later, at the end of the Revolutionary War, Washington sought nothing more than to return home to Virginia. The war for independence won and the British troops all but departed from New York, Washington and his top officers gathered for one last evening together at a Manhattan tavern, during which the General addressed his men for the final time as their commanding officer. None of them knew at the time, although some may have suspected, Washington would later become the first president of the United States and Commander in Chief of the new nation's military forces.

That evening, however, Washington's now-famous final address was as earnest as it was brief.

"With a heart full of love and gratitude, I now take leave of you. I most devoutly wish that your latter days may be as prosperous and happy as your former ones have been glorious and honorable," Washington told his men.

---

10 *Valley Forge.* Bob Drury and Tom Clavin; Simon & Schuster, 2018.

"I cannot come to each of you but shall feel obliged if each of you will come and take me by the hand.[11]"

It is a further testament to Washington's commitment to his men and to his cause that he was able to overcome abysmal supply chain conditions, inhospitable weather, and other physical elements as well as underhanded political maneuvering within his own ranks while leading the nation to independence. In fact, some of the men present that final evening may very well have been in cahoots with the few dissenting parties who sought to have Washington removed during the winter at Valley Forge.

Yet Washington's accomplishments further demonstrate what one can accomplish with the right attitude and a loyal and committed team that shares the same resolve as its leader.

Such loyalty and commitment were central to my early success as well. I was fortunate when first starting out in my own practice to have met a young physician's assistant who was looking for a job. Don Bulla joined my team 34 years ago and is still with me today as Vice President of Bethany Medical. He is the face of the company; he manages and trains new providers and is responsible for their welfare.

Don is there seven days a week, in good times and in bad, and although we disagree from time to time, we share a commitment to one another and to the community of team members and patients whom we serve. Our team is built around how we relate to each other, protect each other, and defend each other in our respective absences. He and I trust each other implicitly, and we know each other's minds. So, when leadership is required, or there is an issue that one of us would normally tend to but cannot, he or I can step in on the other's behalf and, with the same respect and loyalty from our team members, the situation is handled. This example is reflected at

11   *George Washington's Farewell Toast.* Lynn Price, www.washingtonpapers.org, 2018

every level of the company and is rooted in the singular theme of this chapter—commitment.

The great revolutionary-turned-humanitarian and world leader Nelson Mandela spent 27 years in prison for attempting to lead his people and all people in South Africa out of Apartheid. The racial discrimination, subjugation, and violence there took root at the turn of the 20th century and worsened decade by decade until about the middle of the century when the rest of the world began to take note. Personal prejudices and social distinctions became law, and the further dehumanization of the indigenous people, the segregation and oppression backed up by forced poverty, harsh labor, and horrific violence became too much to stand.

Mandela, a self-proclaimed country boy[12] who was the first of his family to receive proper schooling, had some legal training and he began to fight back. What began with work stoppages and peaceful protests soon gave way to sabotage and clandestine strikes against the occupying racist government.

Without recounting the entire saga of perhaps the darkest time in another nation's history, or perhaps the world's for that matter, Mandela was imprisoned on Robben Island, sentenced to life and forced labor. Yet he did not give in. Mandela continued to call for the end of Apartheid, and after nearly 30 years of mounting pressure from South African groups and political opposition parties, as well as the outside world, Mandela was eventually released from prison.

It would not be long before voting rights and other measures were initiated, and in short order, Mandela was elected president. Vowing he would serve only one term, Mandela set about enacting a policy of unification, forgiveness, and equality for all people. There had been great

---

12 *Long Walk to Freedom.* Nelson Mandela; Little, Brown Publishing, 1994

fear that if the Black population ever took power, they would subjugate the Whites with as much or more ferocity as they had been subjected to. Mandela instead brought together his divided nation and, in many ways, the world. And he kept his word, stepping aside after one term yet remaining on the world stage as an advocate for peace, unity, and equality the world over.

Again, what a testament to the idea of total commitment to one's beliefs and ideals. Mandela is now a name synonymous with unification, liberation, and freedom. A man dedicated his life, was willing to *sacrifice* his life, if need be, and despite being imprisoned for 27 years, never stopped working toward the idea in which he believed so fervently and whole-heartedly.

Imagine the company or business you might build in 27 years with that same level of commitment. Envision the impact you might have on your community with that level of dedication and involvement. I often hear people say they have a great idea or big dreams and aspirations, if only they had the time, money, or the right people behind them. If only the system weren't stacked against them, if only there was better access to education, funding, or what have you. I agree. There ought to be those things and more, and I know some very smart and committed people in the Triad are working on those very issues, and they do have their work cut out for them.

Still, there are people in the world who have come from worse places than you or me, overcome bigger obstacles and greater disadvantages, and accomplished far more. Therefore, I encourage you—as I have and often still do—to look to the people who came before us and who achieved so much with so little against greater odds than those that you or I must face, and find that strength, courage, and commitment within yourself to press forward.

Not only should you locate and identify this engine of determination and grit inside of you, but cultivate it, foster it, and share it with others. When you believe in your dream, others will believe in it too. And you will be surprised at how far you will go with a good team who is committed to "the cause" as their leader: you!

> "The quality of a person's life is in direct proportion to their commitment to excellence, regardless of their chosen field of endeavor."
>
> **Vince Lombardi**

PRINCIPLE #6 TAKEAWAYS

- Commit 100 percent to your own success.
- Select and cultivate team members who share in your vision and level of drive.
- Develop the tunnel vision needed to filter life's distractions.
- Don't be shy about communicating your goals to the team; foster the camaraderie needed to get the job done.

SECTION III
INNER RESOURCES

"We are living in a time of uncertainty, anxiety, fear, and despair. It is essential that you become aware of the light, power, and strength within each of you, and that you learn to use those inner resources in service of your own and others' growth."

ELISABETH KÜBLER-ROSS

PRINCIPLE #7:

HUMOR

"A sense of humor is part of the art of leadership, of getting along with people, of getting things done."
DWIGHT D. EISENHOWER

The most successful among us possess the ability to marshal our inner resources and native personality characteristics to motivate teams (as well as ourselves) and reach the loftiest of goals.

Here, in Section III, we'll explore the role of inner resources such as humor, frugality, wisdom, and sense of spirituality in our path to success.

First, let's take a look at humor. Some of you may think: "Humor? In a book about principles of success? Isn't that a bit, um, off-topic?"

My answer, emphatically, is NO! It is very much to the point.

You have probably heard the old saying: laughter is the best medicine. A cliché, perhaps, yet I can tell you with all certainty that it is true. Trust me; I am a doctor.

Of course, as with any medication prescribed these days, the application of humor includes a laundry list of side effects or contraindications, so be advised. In these days of cancel culture, a poorly timed or inappropriate joke may lead to early termination, unintended backlash, irritable acquaintance syndrome or IAS , lawsuits or, in severe cases, death. (OK, perhaps not physical death, but if no one laughs at your joke, you might momentarily feel like you are dying inside!)

However, it is true that being funny does include some level of risk. Humor is quite subjective, and what is funny to some may not be comical to others. Let's face it, cancel culture exists whether some like it or not. And that is precisely the reason why some high-profile comics—Jerry Seinfeld, Chris Rock, and even young Pete Davidson (to name just a few)—will no longer play college campuses; such gigs are simply too fraught.

Nevertheless, a great way to connect with people you are meeting for the first time is by introducing levity. No, no. Give them your real name. Especially if you have an accent like mine, if you are introduced to someone and say, "Hi, my name is Levity," they may wind up calling you that for the rest of the evening.

Seriously though, if you find you can make people laugh, it generally does make the difficult task of meeting new people or engaging in small talk (bleh!) a bit more bearable.

For many people public speaking is truly one of the scariest endeavors that can be undertaken. There is even a medical term for the affliction, *Glossophobia*. According to the National Social Anxiety Center , some 73 percent of the population suffers some degree of public speaking panic, which is tied directly to our inherent fear of rejection.

The good news is that humor can be the balm that wins over the toughest audiences. The psychology of humor—which happens to be the title of numerous books on the subject—is considered "rich grounds for study," according to the Association for Psychological Science. In one account, a 2017 article entitled *The Science of Humor is No laughing Matter*, writer Alexandra Michel[13] offers an engrossing, albeit non-comedic exploration of various scientific studies regarding laughter and comedic timing. Humor is such an integral aspect of interpersonal relationships that researchers have the ability to listen in on a pair of laughing individuals and determine, with roughly 75 percent accuracy, whether the two laughers are friends or strangers.

In a classic TV sitcom, "The Dick Van Dyke Show," one particular episode depicts head comedy writer Rob Petrie (Van Dyke) explaining how comedy works to his son's grammar school class. His scholarly analysis is met with blank stares from the kids. Switching gears, Rob does a bit of slapstick with predictably uproarious results from his son's classmates.

Or, as showbiz veterans are fond of saying, "Dying [on stage] is easy; *comedy* is hard."

Humor can be likened to "the Swiss Army Knife of emotions." We humans are adept at inferring quite a bit of information through laughter. Humor helps us manage stress and understand difficult subject matter.

One way to get over those pre-presentation, public speaking jitters, and instantly connect with your audience is through humor. A quick one-liner might open things up if you're up to the task and have the timing. My generation will most likely remember comedian Rodney Dangerfield, famous for his "I don't get no respect" shtick. For anyone interested in learning to deliver one-liners with impeccable timing, I suggest visiting YouTube and watching clips of Dangerfield on *The Tonight Show* with Johnny Carson. In one instance, after lamenting how tiring it is being

13   *The Science of Humor is No Laughing Matter*. Alexandra Michel; Association for Psychological Science, 2017; www.psychologicalscience.org.

married and having children, Dangerfield says he is taking up the new philosophy of looking out for himself.

"From now on, I'm looking out for No. 1," Dangerfield boasts. "Today, I stepped in No. 2."

Set 'em up. Knock 'em down. It is the time-tested formula of funny.

But, yes, one-liners can be a challenge. A better way to go for a novice, at least one that has worked for me, is a funny anecdote that makes you the butt of the joke. Self-deprecating humor, even in the current climate of political correctness, is a relatively safe space to introduce humor.

I will give you a prime example of how I do this, and keep in mind: Although I am comfortable and fond of public speaking, I feel a bit nervous heading onto the stage. Once things get rolling, however, I do tend to calm down and settle in, as have my audiences. This anecdote has helped with that.

I start with a general statement thanking whoever introduced me and also extending gratitude to whoever is sponsoring the event for inviting me to speak, as well as the audience for receiving me. I then admit, up front that I am a bit nervous. I will then put the audience at ease by telling them not to worry, partly for their sake but mostly for mine, I plan on being brief.

That may be worth a chuckle here or a giggle there, but that is not the punch line. I follow that up by immediately taking myself down a peg. Here is a brief recount of how it has gone in the past.

"I admit I am terribly nervous speaking in front of a crowd, which anyone who knows me will say is ironic because I love to talk. I am, as you all might call it, a chatterbox. I have been since a child. In fact, growing up in India, we were very poor. Extremely so. We had no running water, no electricity, and food was very scarce.

"My mother would cook all day long to prepare a meal for us, including me and my older brother. Well, my brother and sister would always seem to gobble up most of the food before I had a chance to eat as much as I was able to or wanted to. And I could not figure out why this was always happening. I'd forget, of course, by the next day and so when we'd sit down to dinner again, I would be just as eager as everyone else at the table to eat. Yet not long after dinner was over, I would be so hungry again, and neither my brother nor my sister seemed to ever have this issue.

"Well, I was also a shy child so for a while I said nothing. But one day I summoned the courage, and I asked my mother why I did not get the same portions as my older siblings? You see, I was certain as the youngest child I was somehow being short-changed. Maybe because I was the smallest, or the least athletic, or perhaps, my mother secretly did not like me very much!"

(Pause here for laughter. Knowing when to pause, timing, is everything in comedy.)

"'Lenny,' she shot back, 'it is your own fault you do not get as much to eat as everyone else. It is the reason you are so skinny, and why you do not grow taller.'" (A small laugh here, hopefully.)

"I was shocked. I said, 'Mother, how is it my fault? What am I doing wrong?'

"She said, 'Lenny, you talk all the time, nonstop, from the time you wake up to the time you come home from school! Then, as soon as you finish your homework, you talk all evening long until it is time to go to sleep.

"Maybe if you talked less and chewed more you would get more to eat.'" (Pause for laughter.)

"Well, I was no longer offended when she said that. I was humbled, and better informed. That is when I stopped talking so I could eat more, which is how my public speaking career ended. And I can assure you, I talk so little now at meals that my guests have to ask me what's wrong!"

(Pause for more laughter)

Usually, the audience is well into a good long laugh by now. To cap it off, I may pat my belly and say that recently I have not been missing many meals.

From then on, the audience is in the palm of my hand. They have laughed and seen me laugh. They know a lot more about me than they might have when I first came onto the stage, and they know I can take a joke directed at myself. It disarms the audience and provides them with emotional permission to accept my messaging for the remainder of the presentation.

Another thing this particular anecdote accomplishes is it imparts a subliminal message to the audience. This story recalls a genuine lesson I learned when my mother said those seemingly harsh and, in hindsight, comical words to me. I did talk too much, and I never gave a thought to what others had to say or sometimes even how they were responding to the things I was saying. I learned then to speak less and listen more. As I have recounted in an earlier chapter, this is a powerful tool in both business and relationships. Listening, not just waiting for one's turn to talk but genuinely hearing and processing what others are saying gives us the chance to learn the speaker's mind, what is important to him or her, and what they are truly trying to gain out of whatever is being discussed.

History is replete with instances of successful people incorporating humor into their repertoire. Some you may immediately consider and others you might not have expected to have a funny bone in their body. For example, no one might immediately call to mind former British Prime Minister (1979-90) Margaret Thatcher as someone who left crowds in stitches. For those opposed to her politics, she more than likely did not, since she was widely known as the *Iron Lady*. Still, that does not mean she never cracked wise or slipped one in, earning a fair response from her intended audience. Quite the opposite. The Baroness-turned-career politician had quite the silver tongue with which she simultaneously struck down dissenters and brought the proverbial house down in raucous laughter.

One of her more memorable quips came on October 10, 1980, during a speech delineating her counter-inflationary policies. In it, she hammered her opposition and the media of the day who apparently expected she would reverse course. Not one for backing down, whether against Cold War-era Communist Russia from whom her Iron Lady moniker was born or her own parliament members of opposite parties, Thatcher[14] managed to turn the tables.

"To those waiting with bated breath for that favorite media catchphrase, the 'U' turn, I have only one thing to say: 'You turn if you want to. The lady's not for turning ,'" Thatcher said.

Hers was a minor pun, but punchy enough to drive the point home. Those who thought her either too soft or too stuffy were both wrong, and so too in her mind were her political opponents.

Men often underestimate women in positions of power. This is true in politics as well as in business, but having an older sister, I can also tell you this is sometimes true in the family setting. My sister, Gladis, was not to be underestimated, however. She is quite accomplished as a marine biologist, as is her husband, a pediatrician, and both were able to take early retirement after working outside of the country for many years.

This made me pause briefly when I considered approaching Gladis about 15 years ago to ask her to help me with something. The Lenny Peters

---

14 *The Lady's Not for Turning.* Margaret Thatcher; 1980. https://www.margaretthatcher.org/document/104431

Foundation was getting up and running with our home for boys in India, and a home for girls at the time was in the planning stages. I traveled to India to help facilitate some of the more intricate parts of setting all that up, and I immediately recognized that I would need someone on the ground full-time to manage the Foundation's local efforts. I thought of Gladis as my on-site project director, yet I knew she would take convincing.

When I met with my sister in her home, I said to her, "Gladis, I want you to come work for me."

"Lenny, why would I do that?" she asked. "It's not as if I need the money."

"No, no. You did not hear me," I said. "I said I want you to work for me. I did not say I was going to pay you."

We both laughed and from that point forward our conversation was much softer, and we reached an agreement rather quickly. Gladis needed very little convincing after all, and to this day my sister has done a phenomenal job caring for so many children and the less advantaged through our Foundation.

Comedy is not easy. Your favorite stand-up comedians have spent years in front of audiences honing their material in third-rate venues with sparse, disinterested audiences. They battled crippling stage fright and bombed. A lot.

But they got up and did it again, and again, polishing their "tight fives" (a perfected five-minute stand-up) in dives, for a pittance.

Most stand-up comedians never make it. Fear not, you do not have to set out to earn a million-dollar one-hour comedy special on Netflix; you just need to break the ice and get over those pre-speech butterflies. Where you do want to find similarity with the seasoned veterans of the stage is that you must practice. Learning a joke and learning to deliver laughs are not the same.

I recently watched a TED Talk by speechwriter, author, and public speaker Al Wiseman. Wiseman developed, over years of speechwriting and public speaking, a philosophy he turned into a book called *Finding the Funny*[15]. In his TED Talk, Wiseman imparts methods by which he himself learned to find humor in daily occurrences and turn them into fodder for his speeches. He recommends embellishment as a device by which an ordinary routine event can be comedically enhanced in the course of a day. He begins by telling the audience about an old, beat-up car he used to drive. He describes the vehicle in some detail and earns a few laughs, but the payoff comes when he adds the following line:

"Every time I drove this car, tow trucks would be circling me like vultures," Wiseman said.

Of course, this did not actually happen, but it paints a vivid visual of just how beat up the car was and how looking back he can now laugh at the experience, and he invites the audience to join him. Wiseman turned the experience into a speech that won first place in the annual Toastmaster's competition in Georgia. Adding humor to a lecture, or simply learning to identify and deliver humor to whomever you are addressing, be it an audience, a staff or team meeting, or your family seated around the dinner table, has the same effect when pulled off properly. Well-executed humor makes the speaker more entertaining, more relatable, and more well-liked.

Again, there is no need to worry if you are not someone to whom humor comes naturally. Something as hokey as a joke book or Googling the year's Top 10 Dad Jokes will do the trick. You might even try the old bait and switch. Try a non-joke, joke. Something to the effect of the following:

"I told my wife I was going to break the ice this evening with a joke. She begged me desperately not to. My wife doesn't think I'm funny at all. She

---

15 *TedXDecatur: Finding the Funny*. Al Wiseman; 2019.

also doesn't think I know about her secret stash of Oreo cookies stuffed into the three-year-old Raisin Bran box in the pantry, so that shows how much she knows!"

And there it is, you have now earned a laugh with a joke about your own perhaps real, perhaps perceived inability to be funny. Humor paints us in the hue of humility and humanizes us. It is a sleight-of-hand technique that allows us to appear vulnerable and therefore trustworthy, especially to those who might see us as different or somehow apart from themselves.

Use humor wisely and proportionately, and there is no room, stage, or family game night you cannot conquer. And when all else fails, keep it simple. As the saying goes, "It's not rocket surgery!"

> **"Laughter is the closest distance between two people."**
>
> VICTOR BORGE

PRINCIPLE #7 TAKEAWAYS

- Humor helps you connect with audiences and keep them on your side during presentations.
- Nearly 75 percent of us suffer from presentation panic; you are far from alone.
- Practice your opening presentation gambits until they come naturally; build mental muscle-memory.
- Successful leaders respect the power of humor to marshal hearts and minds needed to attain your goals.

PRINCIPLE #8:

BE FRUGAL

"The way to wealth depends on just two words,
industry and frugality."
BENJAMIN FRANKLIN

Being born poor gave me an early understanding of the importance of being frugal. It was a hard and necessary lesson that became engrained in me, part of my DNA. Without it, I am certain my life would have turned out differently. I may still be a doctor, but owning my own practice, my achievements in commercial real estate development and banking, these might still be the stuff of daydreams and empty ponderings doodled on a napkin in some hospital cafeteria in between patients. No, without the life lessons I received from my mother and from growing up dirt poor and shoeless in southern India, I am sure I would not have been able to apply the wisdom of frugality throughout my life that I am now able to share with you here.

I have mentioned I am from a small village in southern India. It is called Murukkumpuzha (I know, "Sure…easy for YOU to say"), situated in the district of Trivandrum, the capital city of Kerala, on the west coast of the southern tip of the Indian peninsula. In my previous book, *Barefoot to Benefactor*, I describe in detail my early existence here, growing up poor and living relatively carefree in spite of it. Kerala is a place where the beauty and sweltering heat battle each day to steal one's breath away. The lush vegetation and varied landscape stretch from the ocean and shore upland into the mountains. Along the way, fruits, vegetables, and rice grow wild and free, enhancing the landscape with vivid colors and soul stirring vistas and aromas to entice the stomach throughout the year.

Technology and infrastructure have significantly increased in the region since my time there as a boy. Although what I experienced then is not necessarily true for everyone living there today, not much has changed for many. As a child, I shared a humble dwelling with my family, my mother and two siblings, an older brother and sister. My father worked for British Petroleum and was stationed in Yemen where he worked 11 months of the year, coming home to us for only one month. The traditional Indian system is quite different than it is in the West, so the money my father made went mostly to providing for his sister's families and their children. In that same vein, my mother's brothers were responsible for our welfare and the well-being of their respective families. This did not leave much money for us, and so we lived modestly and ate what we could grow or could afford to buy from our neighbors and local growers and fish mongers.

My mother would often bargain with the fish mongers as they would walk through the villages each day calling out, *"meen, meen, meen,"* a Malayalam word meaning they had fresh-caught fish to sell. When my mother had a few rupees to spend, she might go out and examine the fish, inspecting each catch for freshness and plumpness, making sure there was enough meat on the fish to warrant the purchase. Still, the fishmonger would quote her a price knowing she would undercut his quote with a lower offer. This practice of haggling was common and expected, and so she would routinely bargain with the fishmonger bringing the price down from, say, 10 rupees, too high, to five rupees, too low, and they would then settle on seven. The fishmonger would then wrap the fish and hand it to me to carry home. I was five or six years old at the time.

I kept that as part of my DNA throughout my life. Yes, it is nice to spoil yourself with some of the luxuries of life, such as a nice car, house, or vacation home. We do not have to sacrifice all luxury and live in poverty or mediocrity. We can be frugal and still enjoy the good things in life, but the way to do so is to *always* try to get the best value for your dollar. This often means striving for the lowest price for the best quality goods and services.

This may seem only logical, yet I know for some people, and perhaps in some cultures, it is an uncomfortable practice. Some people just don't like to negotiate prices. Maybe they are shy. Maybe they feel such negotiation tactics—"haggling"—are somehow "beneath them."

Many times, I have heard someone say that the wealthy are cheap and never seem to want to spend money. Well, there is truth and falsehood in that statement. A wealthy person or someone who has wealth intelligence will always try to get the best value for his or her money because it makes the most financial sense.

For example, let us imagine a person with good credit and high income sets out to buy a car. Should he or she not hunt for the best deal on the make and model of vehicle he or she wants to buy? A person with less money or lower credit might opt for a lower-end car but would still also want to buy it for the best price. Whether buying a Bentley or a Buick, one should not pay more than fair market value, particularly with depreciation and upkeep in mind. It will cost more to maintain and to make repairs on the higher-end vehicle, so the buyer would be best advised to secure the lowest possible purchase price and, if financing, the lowest interest rate.

The same principle should apply to home buying and furnishing your home or office space. He who has the most money won't have it for long if he pays top dollar for every item or service he buys and spends frivolously all over town.

The wealthy take this principle and apply it a step further. We are constantly being approached with "good investments," or being offered the finest quality of a good or service anywhere we go. And yes, we do need to spend money on these items and services to continue to do business and grow and so forth. Yet it only makes good business sense to negotiate the best price for the highest quality items because of the same principles that drive economics or investing—buy low and sell high. The more you save when purchasing, the greater your profit when selling.

When buying a copy machine for your new office you want to make sure it is a high-quality machine that promises minimal down-time and can be repaired easily and cost-effectively. Of course, you want to shop around and educate yourself on the best manufacturers and the most reliable products and service support. Then, within each company, analyze the top tier, second tier, and third tier models of copiers in terms of features and benefits. Now, contrast that information with your needs. Identify whether you need a top-tier, number-one selling model to serve your purposes or if you can make do with the third-tier, number-one selling model. Better still, perhaps the second-tier, second-best selling model serves all the purposes you need filled and is offered at a price that better fits your budget. This is the model you should purchase. Still, what does it hurt to then say to the salesman, or the sales manager if it comes to that, that the product is good and worth purchasing, but the price is too high?

You, the purchaser, are already stepping down from the top of the line, but you are clearly not buying junk. Therefore, you expect you will pay something reasonable for a quality machine, but the advertised price is not in line with the level of quality you have made the informed decision to buy. Maybe there is no room to haggle. Some retailers do have set prices. But they may throw in the extended warranty or add on the three-year warranty for the price of the one-year warranty, which may result in several hundreds of dollars in savings for your company.

Now with that money saved you buy more printer paper than you originally planned, you print up more advertisements or mailers than you originally budgeted, and you reach more customers than you originally estimated you could, increasing your first-quarter sales by a couple of percent. By being frugal with the purchase of your office copy machine, you have made money by attracting more clients and selling more of your product or service.

You can still live a luxurious life by applying the same principles. If you can afford to buy a Bentley, there is no reason not to. Yet you should find the model that suits you for the best possible price. The savings you manage to achieve on the purchase might equate to the cost to insure the vehicle or replace the tires somewhere down the road. You still have a Bentley, and you made a good deal when purchasing it. This is still frugality, and when you apply this method of thinking and behaving with every purchase, big or small, and for your home, family, business, or in spoiling yourself, you will always come away with the best product for the best price, thereby saving money while living well and perhaps making more money on top of that.

As I said, I learned these lessons early from mother as she negotiated better prices with fishmongers and produce growers so she could feed her family the best quality food she possibly could. I took these lessons to heart, and I have applied them throughout my entire career, beginning at the very beginning, when I was still a boy in school.

Completing 10th grade at 14, I took on a project that would influence my lifetime and time again, from medical school to starting my own practice and beyond. It was tradition that a few students of the graduating class would volunteer to organize the graduation festivities, including the food. I had seen previous classes spend wildly on needless extravagances, and the result was lower quality food and a mediocre experience for all who attended. I knew when it was my class' turn to graduate, I could use my resources. I still knew many of the fishmongers and rice growers from my village and was sure I could negotiate top-quality food for lower prices. I volunteered to be on the committee that year that organized the graduation, but I made a deal for myself. I told those in charge that if I could run the program, I could achieve a better quality and more enjoyable experience for everyone for a much lower cost, but if I were to do so, I would keep the profit. They agreed, and that is exactly what took place. I negotiated a good price for the freshest seafood and the best quality produce, and we had a grand feast and celebration for our graduation. And I walked away with a nice sum of pocket money.

This repeated itself later when, in medical school, students were once again selected to run the cafeteria for a year at a time. I again drew on my existing resources and connections and volunteered to take charge. I repeated my negotiations with the fishmongers and growers. By doing so, I kept the food quality much higher for a cost that was much lower. This was for the entire year, so the profit was much more substantial and, even better, ongoing. This time I earned enough money to cover my room and board, easing the burden on my family who had been helping to pay the cost. I was also then able to treat myself a little bit with a sound investment. I bought myself a motorbike, a Czechoslovakian Jawa that I painted bright green. Anyone who saw this bike would immediately know it was mine, and I liked the idea of being noticed. I zipped all over the place on my bright new bike and smiled ear to ear the entire time.

It truly was a sound investment as well as a self-indulgence; I could use my new bike to drive around town and also get back and forth from school to visit my mother and siblings at home. Having my own transportation, of course, made me quite popular among my classmates, and I took great pride in giving friends rides and being seen carving in and out of traffic—there are no traffic signals or stop signs in this region, so I was living quite dangerously by doing so and having great fun as well. I used this increased visibility to make more connections and forge new relationships. I even had a girlfriend, but you will have to go back and read my first book to learn more about that. We will stick here to achieving success.

Being frugal not only let me keep more money for myself, but I was able to spend money on things that made my life easier and more efficient. This is what many people misunderstand about being frugal. While it is true there is some sacrifice required, frugality means keeping more of what one earns and gaining the ability to spend, wisely of course, more on items one needs to make life easier, more efficient, and sometimes also more fun.

My definition of frugal is not saving money to live well later, rather it is saving money *while living well today*. Perhaps you might take a more well-known, well-respected investor's word for it. Perhaps a wealth "guru," worth more than $94 billion will suffice. He is a man who despite his great wealth and financial acumen is also known for being quite frugal.

Warren Buffet , of Berkshire Hathaway, still lives in the home he had built in the 1950s. He is known for his plain attire and appearance, as well as for being plainspoken. And it was he who possibly said it best, and I am paraphrasing, that increasing one's cost of living is not the same as increasing one's standard of living. He also ascribes to the notion that no single investment or wealth strategy is right for every person. Someone aspiring to amass a fortune is going to spend and save in a manner much different from one who only plans to work until retirement and then live off his or 401K and Social Security. The latter might spend more throughout his or her life on taking trips and doing things with or for the family, whereas the former might scrimp and save, investing all he or she can today so that down the road there will be a surplus of money for a higher living standard.

Neither strategy is better or worse, each one is determined to be the right fit for the individual. Yet, within both lies room for frugality.

When I was in London, working as a doctor and continuing my training, I made a great deal of money for a single man in his 20s even while sending the bulk of my income back home to my family. My apartment was paid for and my expenses were low, so I had enough to do as most people will, spoil myself a little bit. Still, I remembered my early lessons in getting the best value for my money, so when I set out to buy a sports car, I wanted one that would serve all the important purposes a sports car should—it should be sleek, stylish, and of course very fast—but would not break the bank. I ended up with a British Leyland Triumph TR7 . I was a foreigner in the country, young and relatively well off, and so this flashy car added to my exotic appeal while also opening doors for me, a dark-skinned, heavily accented immigrant in the mostly White, affluent section of London in which I was living and working. And it did not hurt with the young ladies, either. I was able to negotiate a good price and make a purchase that gave me everything I wanted within my budget.

This was me deciding to spend what I could afford at that time in my life to enjoy a higher quality of life than I had ever known. Later, when I was married and starting a family and my own practice, I would have much different financial goals and a different budget to work with, so a recalibration was in order.

Yet again, being frugal allowed me to meet my new circumstances without overextending myself and getting further and further into debt. I could not risk such a method and jeopardize all I was trying to build so that I could drive a fancy sports car. I knew at that time that if I did what I had to do to establish and grow my business wisely, I would have much more income later to drive whatever kind of car I wanted and it would be paid for in cash, for the best price of course.

To this day, I have preached this policy to my team members within my companies. When ordering supplies or comparing quotes from vendors or contractors, whatever price is quoted, the employee is to react with the following phrase: "Oh my God, that price is too high."

The impetus then falls on the seller to react. If the company stands firm in its price, it may be that the product or service is of a certain value the company deems reasonable and they might not budge. If this is the case, we must decide to pay it or move on to another firm. More likely though, the vendor will ask what price range we are looking to stay within and either the price or the parameters of the deal might be re-examined, and a deal struck that is more beneficial to our interests. There is generally the expectation for negotiations in business deals, large or small, and this is built into the seller or service provider's price setting and marketing. Even when the price is fixed, being frugal might lead to securing a longer contract or a higher gross for the same price. This is still a victory for our company.

Today many businesses have adopted this philosophy, particularly on the internet, where countless websites market products at the lowest advertised price. Consider Amazon or Ebay, for example. These multi-billion-dollar businesses are based on gathering products for low prices, passing the savings on to the consumer and profiting by volume and variety. This did not start with the rise of the web-based marketplace. There first was a shift in the physical market ushered in by a company you might have heard of. In fact, you probably frequent this company's stores without even realizing its role in re-shaping the retail industry. I am talking, of course, about Walmart.

Sam Walton saw his billion-dollar idea begin to take shape in Arkansas in the 1950s. Walton established Walton's 5&10 in downtown Bentonville, Arkansas, shortly after his military service during World War II. [16]

Capitalizing on the success of his multi-goods five-and-dime store, Walton opened the first Walmart in 1962. He was 44 years old. Eight years later, the company went public, and over the next three decades Walmart stores sprung up in cities across the country. Today there seems to be a Walmart anchoring the strip mall at every major intersection in almost every major city in the nation, and even one-traffic-light towns have a location there or in the next town over. The company's stock is up nearly 105 percent over the last five years, which have been a challenging time for lesser retailers, to be sure.

The company attributes its rapid and sustained growth not only to its business model of low-prices and wide variety, but to its team members and commitment to customer service. Of course, there were naysayers along the way, and controversy followed the rise of Walmart as it coincided with or perhaps accelerated the demise of the mom & pop stores in Middle America, but the success of the company is undeniable. And without the buy-in of the consumers whose dollars helped build it, Walmart could not have succeeded. This is precisely the wisdom of what Walton tapped into, frugality. From the consumer trying to keep expenses low, to the vendors being willing to seek profits through lower prices and higher sales volumes, Walmart delivered on all fronts and therefore revolutionized the retail industry. In doing so, Walton built a fortune for himself and a legacy for his

---

16   Walmart Corporate History; https://www.walmartmuseum.com/content/walmartmuseum/en_us/visit/5-10.html

family, still today one of the wealthiest families not only in America but in the world.

I have been able, on a smaller scale mind you, to build a business portfolio and legacy of my own that will for now and far into the future secure a better standard of living for my children, grandchildren, and great-grandchildren. To ensure the legacy continues, I have instilled in my own children the very same lessons my mother passed down to me. While I might have done so negotiating business deals and contracts, even the formation of a successful bank rather than by haggling over the price of fish, the result has been the same. Whether in running the family's business portfolio or in their own individual lives with their respective families and interests, my principles for success have been instilled in my children. Among the foremost on the list is being frugal.

Wherever you are in your own journey, whether in the idea stage, startup phase, or ready to finalize succession, being frugal will better position you to succeed. It will improve the lives and careers of your team members and those to whom they pass on the lesson as well. It is the same as with faith or good morals; the more firmly planted and stronger the root system, the healthier and longer-lived the tree will be.

> **"Frugality is the mother of all virtues."**
> JUSTINIAN

PRINCIPLE #8 TAKEAWAYS

- Frugality frees financial resources for other needed purchases.

- Never shy away from price negotiation. Every seller expects to be asked to "sharpen their pencil."

- Frugality is simply good business sense.

- Being frugal is all about getting the optimal goods or services at the best price. It is not about lowering one's sights on quality and opting for "cheaper" products that ultimately do not deliver superior ROI.

PRINCIPLE #9:

SEEK WISDOM

"I am still learning."
MICHELANGELO

Let's be honest with ourselves: none of us knows everything. No one can, and no one ever will. If we are truly wise, we realize someone else most likely knows what we do not, and from that person we might learn.

Wisdom comes to those who seek it. Consider those whom we think of as wise; of course, our grandparents and parents, but who else? Perhaps gurus and yogis and Kung Fu masters, those who have lived long lives and dedicated themselves to one craft, one art, one philosophy for their entire lives.

We might also look to public and private sector innovators. Titles such as CEO or President often infer attributes that may or may not exist within the person. Still, most will agree it would be difficult for someone to attain such a position without having acquired and applied *some* degree of wisdom.

Conversely, let us consider the small business owner who founds their company and runs it successfully for 30 or 40 years. It is probably safe to imagine this person might have some experience and ingenuity at problem-solving. One day, when the owner is ready to retire and seeks to hand over the business to an offspring or exits through a sale or acquisition, would it not be wise for the new owner to spend time with the former, perhaps a year or more, to seek input and benefit from his or her wealth of institutional knowledge?

Naturally it would, and this is very often the case in the sale, acquisition, or a succession of a business. Before we go deeper into that, let us explore wisdom a bit more. Most textbook definitions arrive at wisdom by mixing in knowledge, reason, and good judgment. So, at the crossroads of being informed, being sensible, and being insightful we find a wise person. How did he or she get there? Those of us who have been on the planet for a few years know well that not everyone who ages are wise.

Wisdom is not part of a package that includes wrinkles, gray hair, bum knees, and macular degeneration.

Wisdom requires experience, both broad and deep. Someone who has "been there; done that" has the experience that can save you time, effort, money, and spiritual pain. They know where the trap doors are and how to avoid them.

And those who have true wisdom can also communicate their learnings well and, thus, hold tremendous value for us lesser mortals.

"True wisdom." I am not referring to the egomaniac blowhards who pontificate on all topics and claim to hold "the answers." Unfortunately, legions of these fakes have overgrown society like cultural kudzu. If you encounter such a person, walk away or risk coming back all the more the fool.

An ancient quote attributed to the sage Lin Chi[17] states, "If you meet the Buddha, kill the Buddha."

Anyone who claims to have all the answers probably has none. The truly wise man knows this, so if you ask him, he might tell you he does not know, trusting you will learn and retain a more valuable lesson through self-discovery.

Returning to our purpose in this chapter—we must learn to recognize the wisdom we lack and foster the ability to know when and where to seek it out when needed.

Once, when I found myself at a crossroads, I called my father seeking his advice. As I said in earlier chapters, my father had worked for British Petroleum for many years, including several years in Yemen from which he only came home for 30 days out of each year. Working for such a large international company and having travelled and lived abroad, my father had insights into some of what I might have been thinking or feeling as I was beginning to travel and live and work in foreign countries. Now, my father being a father, his first instinct was to tell me that if I wanted, I could stay home and work as a doctor in India and marry and keep with tradition. Yet my father knew my heart and that my ambition lay elsewhere, so he quickly let that go and got to the heart of it.

"If they eat snake, you should eat the middle piece," he said.

He was not being literal, of course. What my father meant and what I understood instantly was that if I were to make a go of things and pursue my dreams, whether it be in London, which is where I was at the time, or later in the U.S., to succeed, I must immerse myself in the culture. Dive right in. A more common expression is, "When in Rome,

---

17   Kill the Buddha; Zen Master Dae Kwang; Sept. 30, 1997; kwanumzen.org

do as the Romans do." Yes, there is the inclination to blend in and not stand out as a foreigner, but as my fellow immigrants might attest, when you look and sound as different as I do relative to the naturally born citizens of the U.K. and the U.S., assimilation is easier said than done.

If I were to learn the local lingo, the customs and habits, the popular culture as well as the history and traditions, then I would minimize the chances of running into misunderstandings or embarrassing blunders. One might also discover, as I did, that there is a world of infinite possibility if one can think big and work hard. My father's words have resonated in my head over the years, and I can still hear them today.

"Don't stay outside the culture. Don't be a foreigner all your life. Step inside the system," he said.

I stepped inside and I have been fully immersed ever since.

The wisdom my father imparted to me came from his own experiences and what I will call his acquired knowledge. But it also came from his heart, his love for his child and what I will call his inner knowledge. He did not have to think long or parse his words carefully. He knew what I needed to hear and was able to phrase it in a way he knew I would understand. This is something we as parents and perhaps grandparents know that we often do with our own children. Yet what we might not be aware of is that we also do it with ourselves. Our inner voices know what to say and how to say it when encouraging us to do something or not to do it. And we must listen to our inner selves. There is wisdom within.

You may be familiar with the story of the Buddha, who I referred to earlier in the chapter. If not, here is a condensed version. Long before the widely accepted religion of Buddhism spread through many Eastern cultures, and nowadays some pockets of the West as well, there lived a young prince. Anything the boy ever needed was within his grasp; he need only ask, and it would be granted to him. One day, when he was young man, the prince ventured outside the walls of his home or compound or castle and saw how the other half lived. He saw the wealthy, the middle class and, for the first time, he witnessed poverty, the homeless, and the hungry. He was struck and from that moment sought to understand the root of human suffering and find a solution.

The prince cast off his royal garb and set about traveling the landscape, speaking with people and asking questions, but getting nowhere. Fatigued, he sat under a tree and began to meditate. For 49 days and nights he sat in contemplation, reaching periods of no thought whatsoever, simply being. As he learned to stay in this space longer and longer, he found more and more peace and understanding. Eventually he reached it, the pinnacle of freedom of thought—nirvana. When he awoke, the Buddha—as he would now be called—understood the root of human suffering was attachment, man's desire for possessions and status and belonging. To want or need anything worldly was to suffer until it was obtained, then to suffer under the burden of either not being satisfied with it or the struggle to keep or maintain it.

Freedom from desire or attachment freed the body and mind of suffering. The soul achieved what we would today call *enlightenment*. This is what the Buddha found and eventually convinced his closest followers to seek. They struggled and strived until they too reached enlightenment (or at least, found the right spiritual "neighborhood"). They spread out across the lands to impart the lessons of the Buddha. Today there is an entire religion and thousands of books on the philosophy and teachings of Buddhism and the Buddha himself.

Perhaps one of the most famous practitioners of at least some of the Buddha's teachings is someone also noted for his great leadership and motivational skills. His legacy is near the top of his field if not the peak of it. He has more championship rings (11) as a head coach than anyone else and another two as a player.

The man with more rings than fingers, 13, is none other than basketball's Phil Jackson, head coach of both the six-time championship winning Chicago Bulls teams of the 1990s, and five-time championship winning Los Angeles Lakers teams of the 2000s.

Jackson, raised by parents who were both devout Pentecostals, spent most of his early life rebelling against his family's influence over his spirituality. This compelled him to seek out and study dozens of other world religions and philosophies, including the two which struck a chord with him more than any others, those of the Native Americans of the Midwest and the Buddha. Jackson, in his 2013 book *Eleven Rings: The Soul of Success*, details how his philosophy in coaching and leadership, and moreover, life, was shaped by his life experiences and his mentors. His parents, his coaches, and his self-discovery led to the amalgamation of practices and rituals he amassed and applied in his own life and as a coach. Imagine two of the world's most pre-eminent names in basketball, Michael Jordan and the late Kobe Bryant, the two most driven, most competitive men possibly to have played professional sports, sitting with their respective teams in a room with the lights off, focusing on their collective breathing and bonding as a unit via group meditation. That may sound funny, but it led to championships and personal and team records, achievements, and awards, and to legacies cemented in the form of Hall of Fame careers for so many people affiliated with these teams, players, coaches, owners, and more.

Without Jackson's diligent and ceaseless quest for wisdom, we might not have seen the Bulls dynasty or the resurgence of the storied Lakers franchise that took place under his respective reigns as head coach. Imagine, if you might, Jordan with only a ring or two, and Kobe with one, if any. Unthinkable, is it not? These are two of the most talented and hardest working professional athletes of any sport the world has ever known, and yet without their teammates and Jackson, they might never have achieved the success with which their names are synonymous today.

Talent alone is not enough. Hard work on its own is not enough. Desire and commitment contribute success but do not secure it, not alone. It takes a level of mental and spiritual buy-in, coupled with the hard work and discipline employed to cultivate the existing talent and forge camaraderie and trust required to rise to the championship level. Jackson found ways to get his players, individually and as a collective team, to lean into his teachings. Together, they worked towards a "greater good" and, from that, found success.

What this indicates to us is that you can be the best doctor or dentist or mechanic or cupcake baker in three counties, but to build up your practice or business you will need a strong team with a unified belief in what you are building. You will need to empower these employees to do their individual jobs and meet their personal responsibilities so that the team covers all its bases and learns to anticipate problems and obstacles and create solutions of their own to mitigate them. This must come from a singular philosophy geared toward the successful implementation of not only your business model, but your mission statement and your commitment to your clients, patients or patrons, and your surrounding community. You will need strong relationships with your vendors, attorney, and accountant, neighboring businesses, and surrounding residential neighbors.

And whether, like Jackson, it is through Buddhism and Native American teachings or philosophies, or like me, it is rooted in the Christian faith imparted back in India by my mother, or through your own religious or non-religious self-discovered philosophy, there must be a foundation of philosophy and wisdom on which you and your team can rely. Without it, you will have a company of individuals seeking to fulfill individual goals and desires and you will see your team pulled in several directions at once. Although you might achieve some measure of success, you will not grow and succeed to your full potential.

I found this to be true when I first purchased my practice from its previous owner and founder, Dr. N. Hampton Chiles. When he agreed to sell me his practice, a key condition of the sale was that he would stay on as a physician for two years. He knew that his institutional knowledge would be invaluable. Yes, of course, another factor was that he was not yet ready to retire and give up seeing patients. He was applying wisdom to a situation that I, a first-time business owner and relatively new doctor, was too much of a novice to see until later.

Dr. Chiles' wisdom was two-fold. By staying on as a practicing physician, he would be on hand, available to me should I need his insight as to how to run the business. As I have said, when I first started out, I knew nothing of billing and collections, of payroll and labor laws. I had no institutional knowledge to fall back on, and so Dr. Chiles' staying on provided me with a living library.

Also, since he did not yet want to retire, he would continue to see patients. As I was young and fresh out of medical school and having been conducting research and authoring medical papers, I had knowledge of the latest procedures, the most recent innovations in diagnoses and treatment of illnesses, and I knew how to operate the latest equipment. This was the late 1980s and computers were revolutionizing all facets of medicine. I could assist Dr. Chiles in these areas, and, in turn, he could provide me with the sound and sage truisms of medicine that, despite all the technology and innovative ideas in methodology in the world, experienced physicians inherently know because they've seen it. Experience, again, is perhaps the most crucial component in the accumulation of wisdom. It is, therefore, a key ingredient in success and ought not be overlooked, wherever it might exist.

Dr. Chiles could have easily dismissed me as a hot shot new doctor out to prove himself, but instead he recognized that I had some wisdom of my own. Sure, I had nowhere near his wealth of knowledge and experience, but I had the latest training and technological knowledge. Perhaps you have now or will one day have new college graduates or interns working for you. What they lack in experience as it relates to being in the workforce or in your particular field, they may make up for in bringing new skills, new energy, and fresh perspectives to your team.

Sometimes the old way of looking at problems prevents us from discovering or implementing new solutions which may be required in an evolving landscape. Encouraging younger team members to speak up and share their ideas will benefit both the employee and the company as both are given room to inform one another and to grow.

Indeed, wisdom is a two-way street. Billionaire Jeff Bezos, the former CEO of Amazon who took the once online bookstore and built it into the web-retail giant that it is today has many times recounted the fact that much of what he knows about business he learned working alongside his grandfather on the family ranch. In numerous anecdotes, Bezos divulges stories from the Texas ranch his grandparents owned and worked themselves. The wisdom young Bezos obtained from his family's patriarch included life lessons as well as how to conduct business and be as self-reliant as possible.

It was during one of these segments, a story aired on CNBC a few years ago, that Bezos related his childhood education to how he manages his business empire in adulthood. He compared the benefits of being almost entirely self-sufficient as a rancher and doing most everything—from birthing calves to fixing fences and repairing drainage pipes—with relying on the abilities and expertise of one's team in the business world. Wisdom, again, can spring up almost anywhere, within you and without you, as the Beatles famously sang.

"… You get into the business world and anything you do on a team, you very quickly realize that it's not just about your own resourcefulness and that it's about team resourcefulness," Bezos said in that interview. [18]

Wisdom, when it comes down to it, is the application of knowledge in a purposeful manner. It is the ability to strategize and set in motion a series of events that work in your favor.

A chess master must possess more than an understanding of the rules of the game and the moves the pieces on the board are permitted to make. He or she must understand human behavior and be able to tell if his opponent is patient or makes hasty decisions. In chess, one must consider strings of moves and counter moves, with tactics based on a variety of factors. It is the ultimate strategy game, necessitating that the player be capable of thinking three, four, or five moves ahead at any time throughout the match.

There are of course phenoms and savants, those with a seemingly inherent ability to play the game extraordinarily well and defeat even the most seasoned opponents. Yet for most of us, as with anything else, chess requires practice and lots of it. It requires continually playing opponents of increased skill and experience so we, in turn, sharpen our own skills and develop more strategic experience.

Success in life and in business is also like this. Some people, no matter where on earth they are born or under what conditions, will succeed no matter the odds. The rest of us are grinders, and we have to practice, study, and continue to seek out new mentors and undergo new and varied experiences. Only then can we begin to accumulate the know-how as well as the resources to succeed.

18   "What Jeff Bezos Learned About How to be Successful Working on his Grandfather's Ranch as a Kid." CNBC; May 14, 2018.

Hence this book. I may have been one of those fortunate people who from birth could have succeeded. Maybe, to a degree. For me to achieve the success levels I strive for, I must continue to grow, learn, and gain experience.

I still seek wisdom even at this stage in my life. I find it in those who came before me, those who are journeying alongside me, and those who are following in my footsteps while charting their own course.

Wisdom springs forth from the most unlikely places. We must never hold such stringent beliefs or allow ourselves to be so biased that we discount the ability of anyone, regardless of race, sex, religion, orientation, or status to teach us something we do not know.

The new hire, the janitor, or the doorman may utter the phrase or point out the subtlety that gets the wheels turning and leads to the Eureka moment that proves the difference in the project you are currently involved in reaching a successful conclusion. Keep your senses open to the world around you and to the voice inside you. Call it instinct, call it the Universe guiding you, or call it Divine intervention, but whatever the source, the wisdom we seek is often all around us.

Lastly, it never hurts to be the source of wisdom for someone else. Pay it forward, as the expression goes. If you encounter someone seeking wisdom and you just so happen to know the solution or where to find it, there is no harm in nudging the person along the right path. The energy you put forth into the world you receive back 100-fold. I resolutely believe this, and I practice it in my own life.

It costs nothing to be kind and only time to impart to another person what you have learned along your journey, yet the rewards you might reap and satisfaction you will achieve by seeing that person succeed will far exceed what you have spent. Seek wisdom wisely and you will not go astray.

> **"Wisdom is the application of knowledge."**
>
> DR. LENNY PETERS

PRINCIPLE #9 TAKEAWAYS

- Wisdom is the purposeful application of knowledge.
- Seek out wisdom from your elders, your peers, and from younger people; no one age group has a monopoly on wisdom.
- Run, don't walk, away from those who would have you believe that they are the font of all knowledge.
- Accept the gift of wisdom when honestly rendered. If Michael Jordan and Kobe Bryant can embrace the team-first wisdom of their coach, so can we.

PRINCIPLE #10:

IT'S GOD'S TEAM

"Sir, my concern is not whether God is on our side; my
greatest concern is to be on God's side,
for God is always right."
ABRAHAM LINCOLN

No one can achieve significant success alone. We need a team. As the saying goes, it takes a village to raise a child. Successful people assemble great teams to accomplish their goals. In any field of endeavor, from the worlds of sports, politics, commerce, and academics, the best of the best attract and retain superior individual talents and then mold them into great teams.

Whether it was gaining independence or holding itself together by its seams, or even stepping in as the world twice sought to tear itself to shreds, America is perhaps the world's greatest example of team-oriented success. Now, we are not revisionists as we have already committed to stop lying to ourselves, so we must concede there are portions of America's story that we must continue to confront and rectify. Such is life.

As an immigrant, I have experienced our nation's promise firsthand, as well as its growing pains. I reflect now on the beauty of that sentiment not as an assault on the character of the nation but rather as an acknowledgement that it indeed lives up to its promise. I do believe the nation is as it was described by the faithful founders, Providence, a beacon on a hill, a guiding light divined by God.

As such, if the U.S.A. represents the greatest team the world has ever known, that is because it is a nation truly greater than the sum of its parts. America endures, because of its commitment to live up to its founding principles. We continue to reshape ourselves and evolve. And, yes, it is not an easy task.

And while they may have been Christian in faith, as am I, the door was left open for all faiths to be celebrated and expressed without discrimination. I maintain then, that as we discuss this country's success or our individual success first as citizens and as families and communities and then in business, each of us is a member of the same team—not of our own construct, but of God's or of the Universe's.

Drilling down, we arrive where we began, that successful people achieve in large part due to the successes of their respective teams. In the world of sports, there always seems to be a dynastic cycle. In football, there are the Green Bay Packers of the 1960s, the Pittsburgh Steelers of the '70s, the San Francisco 49ers of the '80s, and, most recently, the New England Patriots.

In basketball, we have seen the Lakers, the Celtics, the Bulls, the Spurs, and others each make multiple championship runs. And in baseball, who can we look to but the New York Yankees, with 27 championships, far and away more than any other franchise across all major sports. Each of these teams had owners, front office personnel, and staff before any player, manager, or coach took to the field or the court. General managers assemble the teams, and coaches and managers lead the players game-by-game from training camp to the end of the season and, hopefully, to the hoisting of the championship trophy.

In business, we must look at the components of a championship team, preferably a dynasty, and emulate that. As owners and CEOs, we must make sound investments and secure hires , not only adding the best people to our team but empowering them to do what we hire them to do and arming them with the necessary tools to succeed. Yet we cannot possibly find ourselves in the position to do so, or in the graces of the Universe to find and land the best candidates, to trust and encourage the leadership and execution of our team members without trusting that God puts us all together and makes us capable. He affords us the opportunities.

For example, when I began to expand my practice and form Bethany Medical, I was fortunate to receive my Vice President Don Bulla, the first person to join my team. This was more than 30 years ago, and he remains with me today, supporting, strategizing, executing. He is constantly training new team members and helping existing team members grow in their roles and lives.

My other Vice President, Patrick Watterson, has been with me for the last 25 years. He remains an integral part of the team, training new members, proposing new ideas, and challenging my own vision. Sometimes we disagree, although always in private, and that's OK. It's a dynamic tension that has worked to our mutual benefit; Watterson has helped build the rest of the team of top managers to help us grow from a doctor's office in High Point, North Carolina, to become the largest independent, single-owner healthcare provider in the state of North Carolina.

In fact, we have recently discovered and are in the process of verifying that we are now the largest minority-owned business in North Carolina, followed by Michael Jordan and the ownership group behind the

National Basketball Association's Charlotte Hornets, Hornets Sports and Entertainment.

This might be the first time Michael Jordan has come in second place!

Through massive and unpredictable changes in healthcare over the last 35 years, my team and I have stood together while our competition has either been bought out or gone bankrupt. This is as much a credit to my team and why I continue to depend on them today.

My daughter, Elise, four years ago, stepped into the role of President of our seven companies. She is charged with leading our team now and for the next 30 to 40 years, as I am taking a lesser role over time, and she continues to take on more responsibility.

Our team is driven by our faith and thankful for all of our blessings. We are motivated by creating jobs, growing our companies, and helping those in need here in the U.S. and around the world. We believe we are doing God's work. It is not our work that we do, but His, and we will go as near or as far and commit as much or as little as we are led to.

I understand not everyone is religious or holds as closely to his or her faith as I do. If you are not a person of faith, consider the factors that guide you in your own life. Perhaps it is the Universe, or Mother Nature, or the Grand Design and the energy or entity which exists behind that force. Consider your ancestors or Karma, whatever it might be that not only motivates you but compels you to go forward and opens doors or surrounds you with blessings.

A few years ago, while I was expanding my businesses and looking to take on greater challenges in healthcare, financial services, and real estate, I prayed. For you, maybe there is meditation or a hobby that you engage in to clear your mind. If so, pursue that and make it part of your daily life. For me, there is meditation and prayer.

On this occasion I prayed, and I asked for guidance in putting the right people around me to help my team succeed as we pushed forward. I asked for help building the right team so that we could grow and continue to help His people, those who could not help themselves such as orphaned children or the sick and dying, even those experiencing temporary hardships. I asked that we be able to give them a hand when needed.

I heard a voice say back to me, "You do not have a team. It is my team; I simply asked you to lead it."

In the months and years that followed, many competent and highly qualified people joined our team. Many of these folks seemed to spring up from nowhere, coming to us rather than us seeking them out. They joined our team and have helped propel us toward financial success and, equally important, our calling in serving our fellow humans.

My sister Gladis is an excellent example. She has master's degrees in marine biology and zoology and spent a portion of her career teaching at the university level in India. She married a doctor, and together they left India to work in several other countries, and in the process, became financially independent. She may not be "rich" by American standards, but she is very well off by Indian standards with two homes, one in the city, one in the village, two servants, and two drivers.

Around the same time that I heard what I believe was God's voice telling me the team I would lead is His and not mine, my sister and her husband had recently retired and returned to India.

I had already begun establishing the Lenny Peters Foundation and organizing the home for boys and home for girls in my native India. That is when I went to visit Gladis, and as I recounted in Chapter 7, I asked her to work for me and she said she did not need to work for me, she had her own money. I responded humorously, saying that I never mentioned I was going to pay her.

She did come along with me and take charge of the Lenny Peters Foundation's interests in India. Right away, she showed her commitment and the degree of her inspiration. Since she became President of the Foundation in India, many more volunteers and staff members with degrees and stellar resumes have left their previous posts and come to join our team.

Thus have been the experiences in my life. I set out to build something and almost immediately, seemingly by chance, I was introduced to the right people who saw my vision, shared my goals, and joined our team. I have since come to call these people the angels in my life, each of whom I believe was placed there by God. This has shaped my thinking about teams and why I am so ardent in my faith that our team, our vision, is being led by a Higher Power.

Vince Lombardi is one of the most renowned and accomplished head coaches in the world of professional sports. Beginning in 1959, Lombardi coached the Green Bay Packers to five NFL championships and two Super Bowl victories. A devout Catholic, Lombardi coached as he lived, demanding from himself first the strong faith, discipline, and hard work he demanded of his assistant coaches and players.

He is known for so many quotes, perhaps the most famous being, "Winning isn't everything; it's the only thing."

There is, however, another quote which is both longer and I think more representative of the true measure of the man.

"When we place our dependence in God, we are unencumbered and we have no worry," Lombardi said. "In fact, we may even be reckless, insofar as our part in the production is concerned. This confidence, this sureness of action, is both contagious and an aid to the perfect action. The rest is in the hands of God…the same God who has won all His battles up to now."

For me, I take this to mean that once we admit the world and everything in it is out of our hands and safely in God's, then we are free to take on the challenges and goals we in our own lives hope to pursue. If we trust, He will take care of the rest, and we can move freely toward our own success.

Again, my faith does not need to be yours. As we mentioned in an earlier chapter, Phil Jackson, who is one of professional basketball's most revered and successful coaches, used Buddhism and Native American teachings to inspire his players. He and his Chicago Bulls teams of the 1990s twice won three consecutive championships. His Los Angeles Lakers also accomplished a three-peat, winning consecutive rings from 2000 to 2002, and then another two in 2009 and 2010.

The late Pat Summitt led the University of Tennessee women's teams to eight national championships and is widely known to have leaned heavily on her faith, as did Jim Valvano who coached the 1983 N.C. State University men's team to victory. Valvano, for whom the Jimmy V Foundation is named, was also devoutly faithful. Each year, the Foundation raises millions to fund research in the fight against cancer, the disease which ravaged Coach V's body and ultimately ended his life.

Valvano's speech upon winning ESPN's 1993 ESPY Arthur Ashe Courage Award, is perhaps one of the most inspiring and emotionally stirring of all time. Faith, family, and team were among the centerpieces of his speech.

Let us recall others whom we have mentioned throughout this book, those whose leadership and decision-making shaped the world we inhabit today. Presidents Washington, Jefferson, Lincoln, and Roosevelt each made choices which helped forge and sustain our nation amid turmoil and tumult that otherwise could have meant the end of the country and perhaps democracy the world over.

Yet they did not do so alone. Each president had advisors, staff, and Cabinet members on whom he relied. So too did U.K. Prime Ministers Churchill and Thatcher.

Each world leader and CEO referenced in this book had a team around him or her, advising and at times challenging their ideas and shaping their decisions. And each of those teams, I submit, was in part formed by God or the Divine energy of the Universe. Nelson Mandela surely had to rely on both his faith and his team of supporters, his wife, and his friends who fought apartheid in his name while he was imprisoned for decades. Once he was released and climbed to the presidency of his nation, Mandela surely was surrounded by a team who contributed to the formulation and execution of the policies he helped enact to heal a nation divided for decades by racial violence and oppression. That is nothing short of the influence of the Divine, I am convinced.

One final example I feel inclined to share comes from closer to home. I have a niece, Susan, with whom I admit I had fairly little contact throughout much of her life. There was never any conflict or indifference between us; we simply lived worlds apart and had little interaction over the years. Such was my surprise then when I received an unexpected call from Susan which happily led to the formation of our two most recent homes for children and families, not coincidentally, I do not think, in Johannesburg, South Africa.

She called me and said, "Uncle, we are ready to start the Lenny Peters home for children here in Johannesburg."

I was shocked. I almost fell out of my chair. This is another great example of someone' joining our team unexpectedly and, as a result, we were able to grow, expand our reach, and make a difference in our world.

In my opinion, no great leader achieved success alone. It is the team that got him or her there. Anyone can lead a great team, assembled by the

Universe and driven by the energy that is all around us and by our love for our community and those in need. We humans are driven by our great love for others, for our deep-rooted need to help, and by our calling to create wealth. In my personal experience, our team is driven by our faith, and I am simply providing the leadership to God's team.

> **"If you're on God's team, you can't lose."**
>
> JOE GIBBS

PRINCIPLE #10 TAKEAWAYS

- Faith frees us to do our best work for the greater good of our fellow man.
- We are all, ultimately, on God's team.
- Through Him, we can realize our dreams of success, whatever they may be.

BONUS PRINCIPLE #11:

FIND THE LOVE

"To love oneself is the beginning of a lifelong romance."
OSCAR WILDE

As you have learned in this book and my earlier work, my ascendancy from poor street kid in South India to successful American entrepreneur has been a steady and sometimes painful progression. With the help of God, and the collaboration of immensely talented family members, friends, and colleagues, I accomplished more than that street kid could have ever imagined.

It wasn't easy, and I took my lumps. I persevered and doors opened. But when all was said and done, when I look at the P&L statement of my life, in totality, I came to this elemental conclusion: Love is the greatest accomplishment one can achieve.

It is both the foundation and the culmination of success. The incontrovertible evidence is all around us. Without love, some of those historical figures whom we have mentioned throughout this book could never have accomplished the feats of greatness for which we remember them. Nelson Mandela forgave his captors and oppressors and convinced a divided nation to heal itself from within based on the strength of their greater commonalities versus their superficial or cultural differences. Mother Teresa healed the sick and cared for the diseased and discarded souls the world over. Winston Churchill braced his beloved nation as it faced destruction at the hands of the Nazis.

Love starts with the ability to love oneself. Of course, as with everything else, too much of anything isn't good for you. There are those who take ideologies or philosophies too far and we call these people extremists. A self-love extremist is someone who considers himself or herself infallible, above the law and indifferent to criticism. They believe they needn't bother with the input of others.

While the narcissist can become successful, and they often do succeed, to varying degrees, their success is typically less sustainable and benefits fewer people.

In my opinion, this is not the sort of success we should aspire to. It may be presumptuous of me, but if you've read this far, I think you and I are kindred spirits on this. Ours is a more gracious and ultimately satisfying brand of success. Ours is a force that ushers others along our same path so that we might teach and inspire and cultivate generational wealth not only for our own families but for our partners, team members, and communities.

And it begins with self-love. Inherent in this self-love is the ability to share, to pour our love into others, and to receive the love others pour into us. When we engage in this reciprocal endeavor knowingly, we strengthen our faith and convictions, and we enhance our ability to think big and harness our will to find a way. It is in that regard that I say love is the connective tissue that unites each of the principles outlined in this book; it is the special sauce of life.

That is why love is the subject of this final chapter. Call it an encore if you will. To me, love, in the grand scheme, is like listening to a playlist of Beatles songs on shuffle. The songs flood us with layers of emotion and memories. Afterward, we listeners are moved to contemplation and, more often than not, inspired. We feel joy, pain, the exuberance of youth, the hard lessons of life. And, too, we are also reminded that these feelings can, in the very next breath, be forgotten, and so, at last, we are wistful.

Love is fragile. It has infinite potential to fail or succeed. Should it fail, we humans gird ourselves, and bravely take the ride again in the hope for a better outcome. If we approach life this way, and business as well, we will ultimately succeed. That is not to say we will win every roll of the dice, but we will be enriched by each experience. We will learn from our mistakes, and we will appreciate bigger and more consistent gains over our careers and our lifetimes.

We will fail better.

If we are to be successful, we must endure the losses, relish the victories, and recommit each time to the next goal before us, whether we have just won or lost. We must love the game.

Loving ourselves is foundational to a successful life. We, of course, love our children, parents, siblings, and spouses. We love our friends and neighbors. These relationships that comprise our families and communities are the bedrock of society, making necessary things like business and commerce. At its core, success first means ensuring the survival of the self and those around us. From there, it takes on an escalation of meanings, arriving practically at our making a way for a better life, an improved quality of living and, in the very American, dare I say *capitalist* sense, the pursuit of happiness.

Love yourself so that you will not live self-destructively. It is not selfish to say that the most important person in the world is you. Consider this:

Life is made up of time, and when your time expires and you are no longer here, then nothing matters. Other than what you have built in your lifetime and what you bequeath in your will, nothing you say or do will persist beyond your time on Earth.

The love we have for our spouses, or our family drives us to support and care for them, to teach and nurture them, and if need be, to put ourselves in harm's way to spare them. Yet, if *we* are not whole, we will not be able to do so. A poor man cannot lend another poor man money. An uneducated man cannot teach another man about finance or physics. And a loveless person cannot love another person until he or she fills their own vessel with love, from which he or she might pour into others.

While it helps to be lucky, success depends so much upon feeling confident, driven, educated and experienced, and wise and insightful. No one who has a hard time loving himself or herself is going to pursue their dreams and ambitions. Those who cannot, or do not, love themselves will be too busy wallowing in self misery and will likely lash out at others. A common phrase in psychology is that "hurt people hurt people," and that people lacking in self-love struggle to initiate and sustain relationships. So, while we must draw the line at narcissism and being egotistical to the point no one will want to work with us or can stand to be around us, we must develop healthy amounts of self-love.

It is simply nourishment that gives us the emotional strength to help others.

Next, we must be honest with ourselves about whether we sincerely love what we do. Business is difficult enough without setting ourselves up for failure. If I hate lemonade, I am probably not going to launch a new line of lemonade' drinks. I might invest in a company that bottles lemonade or that distributes lemon flavors for use in sodas and ciders and such, but I am not going to go spend months working with farmers and chemical engineers and marketing and branding consultants to develop a new citrus beverage and try to carve out my own corner of the lemonade market. That would require so much time and energy being spent surrounded by something I hate, and I would not put my best effort or focus my energy consistently in making sure the new line succeeds. I will become angry and, pardon the pun, bitter, and I will likely quit at the first sign of difficulty.

If you are involved in a business in which you cannot find joy and fulfillment, go and find something else. You are not going to be successful, at least not in the long term, if you do not love what you do. Find something that you like, that you enjoy, and that you can love through the ups and downs and over the span of a career. You will be more apt to invest the necessary time, effort, and energy to see it succeed, and you will be happier and more fulfilled away from work as well.

For us to fully arrive at success we must be as happy in our private lives as we are in our professional roles. It boggles my mind then that in America, where so many people have such potential for success, it seems so many are so willing to be in superficial relationships. According to the American Psychological Association, 50 percent of all marriages in the U.S. end in divorce. That statistic applies to situations in which it is the couple's first marriage. In cases of subsequent marriages, the divorce rate is even higher.

In India the divorce rate is closer to 1 percent. Now, I will concede there are some traditional differences in culture between the two nations, and that it might not be healthy in some cases to stay married, specifically in situations where there is abuse or neglect or even unhappiness. A divorce rate of or below 1 percent indicates there are probably some people staying married for the wrong reasons. Still, a 50-50 shot at success is hardly a gamble one should be willing to take on something as meaningful as marriage. We are talking about an institution that many believe to be holy, one that often results in producing and raising children; one that is inherently a financial and economic partnership. All of these are reasons a couple should be far more assured than 50 percent that their union will last and be fruitful.

I believe one reason American marriages so often end in divorce is that, as a society, we do not educate our children in how to choose a partner. We parents do our best to supervise our children's dating choices and habits while we have them, but after high school we cast them out into the world, be it college or the work force environment, and we say, "happy hunting, choose wisely!"

This is not so in India. There, most marriages are arranged. To this day! I understand that might be unimaginable to my North American and European readers. But in many parts of the world, this is still the custom, and believe it or not, couples whose marriages are pre-arranged still do fall in love. Love, after all, is a gradual progression in a relationship between two people developed over time as trust is established and the two parties come to know one another increasingly well.

This is not the Hollywood or Hallmark version of love at first sight, or an overt romantic gesture performed by one to sweep the other off his or her feet, where it all ends happily ever after. Such story arcs are myths that contribute to the U.S.'s high divorce rate. I am not saying it is impossible, but it is rare that such a marriage lasts and remains happy and fruitful for all involved.

Nor is it accurate to say all arranged marriages are perfect matches and all Indian couples joined in this way are better off for it. Perhaps it is an old-fashioned or conservative ideal, but I believe that vows mean something and that couples who stick through the hard times and come out the other end do so with an appreciation for one another, for the lives they build and share, and for their children and grandchildren. The stability is in the statistics.

Take, for example, my own parents. Joseph Peter, my father, was 10 years my mother's senior. My mother, Philomena Lopez, had since childhood, developed a strong faith and pursued her Christian religion with zeal. Growing up she'd spent a great deal of time in church, devoting her days to prayer, reciting the rosary, and memorizing the Gospel while interacting with the priest. Ultimately, she was forced to give up her ambition of becoming a nun to take on the role of running the post office in our village of Kerala, which had been purchased by her father, my grandfather. Because of her commitments, first to her faith and later to her duties as postmistress, Philomena had no interest in marriage, let alone an arranged match to a man 10 years older than her.

Still, my father came from a good family. Joseph was college educated and had travelled to many cities in India, including Bombay, known today as Mumbai. My mother's objections notwithstanding, my parents' arranged marriage came to pass. Three children would follow, including myself, the youngest. As I have mentioned in earlier chapters, my father went to work in Yemen where he would remain 11 months out of the year. This was the case for most of my childhood, until he retired.

My father's absence put considerable strain on my mother, leaving her alone to manage the duties of maintaining a home and caring for three children, including two very active boys, my brother and me. Also, despite my father's good job with BP, there were constraints on our family's finances. Foremost, unlike in the West, Indian culture is a matrilineal society, meaning the lineage of a family is traced through the maternal side of the family. So, while a man is the patriarch of his own family, he is also charged with the care of his sisters' children as well. My father's sisters had several children, so his duty to provide financially was split among us all.

There was another issue plaguing my parents' marriage: alcohol abuse. My father worked long hours, again separated from his family most of the year. Aside from his paycheck, to compensate for his high-stress position and plight of being stationed a world away from his family, he would often be rewarded by his superiors with bottles of liquor. Over time, my father developed a drinking problem that would sometimes spill over into fits of rage and occasionally violence when he was home. He also grew careless with money when he was in such a state and would either spend liberally at the bar amongst his friends, or worse still, wander home with loose change spilling from his pockets.

Despite all these strains on their relationship, my mother never allowed a disparaging word to be spoken against her husband, not even from their children. She stood by him, so much that once I had attained some success in the U.S. and had a family of my own, I invited my aging parents to come and live with us in North Carolina. They did so, but their stay was cut short when my father, missing his friends back home as well as his drinking time there among them, decided he did not want to live out his days in the U.S. He was intent on returning to India and so he did, along with mother who refused to leave his side.

Within a couple of years, my father had a stroke, followed by another one that left him mostly paralyzed on one side of his body. He could not care for himself and so my mother looked after him to the end. When he eventually passed, only then did my mother return to live with us again in North Carolina, this time staying until her own passing.

Perhaps theirs was not the romanticized tale of enduring affection and whimsical love that one might read about or see in the movies. My parents did, however, raise three highly successful children as well as care for their nieces and nephews and extended families and their community back in Kerala. My mother's faith and my father's strong work ethic and sense of duty, despite whatever flaws he may have had, helped shape me into the man I have become. Their love for me and my brother and sister never wavered, nor do I imagine, albeit perhaps strained at times over his work, his drinking, and their finances, did their love for each other.

Thus, with the right measure of commitment, beginning with the love one generates for themselves and those around them, anything is possible. That love should extend into all things we pursue in life, whether our careers or hobbies, our communities, and our philanthropic efforts. Without this love, we are empty vessels, incapable of pouring into others all we might offer and unable to receive what others might pour into us.

Now that I think about it, love is the common thread of the 10 principles of success herein. It is the fabric that connects us all. Wealth, fortune, and fame cannot truly be categorized as "success" unless it is rooted in love.

> **"All you need is love."**
>
> JOHN LENNON, PAUL MCCARTNEY

MY MESSAGE TO YOU

I wish you boundless success in your personal and professional life. May you be filled with love always, and allow God, The Universe, or whatever Forces you believe in to guide you every day.

DR. LENNY PETERS

LENNY PETERS FOUNDATION

A Helping Hand Here at Home and Around the World

Since 2006, the Lenny Peters Foundation has served as a bastion for those in crisis. For some, the crisis is temporary. For others who are worse off, it is sadly the only life they have known. Despite the varying degrees of need and, in some cases, the thousands of miles of geography between them, the Lenny Peters Foundation exists for all who require assistance, delivering on its motto both locally and globally, to be "A Helping Hand Here at Home and Around the World."

While that takes many shapes, the Foundation's focus has always been two-fold: to provide safety, shelter, and education to those who need it most in some of the poorest pockets of the world and to be a temporary hand-up for those in a more forgiving landscape who might need a little help overcoming unexpected obstacles which have fallen in their paths. Both are answers to a calling from a Higher Power.

On the first front, the Foundation operates 10 homes for orphan children, the sick and dying, the elderly, and prayer centers for the pious—eight in India and two in South Africa.

Secondly, through a digital application process on its website, lennypetersfoundation.org, the Foundation offers one-time financial assistance to individuals and families in need in the Triad region of North Carolina, the Foundation's base of operations.

High Point, N.C., is home to Dr. Lenny Peters, founder and CEO of Bethany Medical and the Lenny Peters Foundation. Bethany Medical, founded in 1987, grew from a single practice with a primary focus on gastroenterology to a multi-specialty health services system with 15 locations, employing 65 providers and more than 500 nurses, medical assistants, administrative and support staff, and more. Today, the company boasts that it is not only the largest independently-owned health services provider in the Triad but also the largest minority-owned business in the state.

After having lived, practiced medicine, and paid taxes on four continents, India, Africa, Europe, and North America, Dr. Peters has developed a wealth of knowledge, experience, and compassion for those who face economic, social, and institutional barriers in life. His journey has been touched along the way by those whom he calls his "angels without wings," people who appeared in his life at just the right moments and offered him the right help he needed at the time. From this, he learned what it means to give, to receive, and that no one succeeds alone.

And succeed he did, albeit through arduous work and strict discipline developed along the way. Dr. Peters believes that from such success comes an ability, and an obligation, to serve one's community. Hence, the Lenny Peters Foundation is an almost entirely self-funded global non-profit 501(c) (3) charity organization.

In fact, 100% of the proceeds from the sale of this book, as well as those from the sale of Dr. Peters' first book, *Barefoot to Benefactor: My Story of*

Faith and Courage, go directly to support the orphan children and cancer patients cared for by the Lenny Peters Foundation.

Dr. Peters attributes his civic inclination to his Christian faith, as well as the influence of his mother, a devout Christian, and his matriarchal grandfather, a sage and source of wisdom during his own life in his family's community in India. Here at home, Dr. Peters has adopted a role similar to his grandfather's, and despite turning over most of his portfolio of businesses in health care, banking, and real estate to his capable daughter, Elise Peters Carey, he remains steadfast in his focus on family, community, and philanthropy.

Truly a family operation, not only does Peters Carey now oversee the family's business interests, but she is also a Board Director of the Lenny Peters Foundation, as are his son, Dr. Anthony Peters, his eldest daughter, Shirin Peters, and his youngest daughter, Nicole Peters.

In addition to the one-time financial donations to those in need, the Lenny Peters Foundation sponsors and supports the programming of dozens of fellow community-minded and civic organizations. In 2021 alone, despite the challenges of an ongoing global pandemic, the Foundation contributed more than $300,000 in philanthropic support to its local community in High Point and the surrounding Triad area.

In 2022, Dr. Peters continued to grow the Foundation's local impact by holding monthly community giveaways, offering much-needed items such as blankets and winter coats in the colder months at the start of the year, to rain jackets and hats during the wet spring season. In the summer, the giveaways leaned into furthering the bond between families, holding events with the local minor league baseball team, and providing desperately needed back-to-school supplies for the start of the new school year in August.

In India, the Lenny Peters Foundation team, led by Director Gladis Eugene, also performs monthly outreach, visiting homes of those in need and delivering financial assistance, prayers, and a welcome visit. Patients afflicted with everything from cerebral palsy to autism and cancer are visited by Gladis, along with Team India staff Ajith Joseph, Feji Anju, and Renjiny George.

The homes operated by the team include The Jayamatha Boys Home; The Lenny Peters Home for Girls; The Lenny Peters Home for Palliative Care; The Lenny Peters Prayer Center; The Lenny Peters Divine Mercy Home; The Lenny Peters Home for Elderly; The Lenny Peters Girls Home; The Lenny Peters Welfare Center for Children; and The Lenny Peters Home for Children.

The team also frequently coordinates with priests and nuns in the local parishes of Trivandrum, the portion of the state of Kerala, India, from which Dr. Peters originally hails, to identify individuals with specific needs the Foundation is well-positioned to assist with.

Bolstered by their strong, individual faiths in God and their genuine desire to serve others, Foundation team members are sometimes deeply affected by their interactions with the community members for whom they care. Many of the families are in severe financial difficulty, and some of their homes are in disrepair. Others still are behind on their mortgages and live in fear of eviction.

Furthermore, many of the people the team visits are in poor health; some are terminal, and others are bedridden. Most do not have health insurance, and many are unaware that the concept exists. Food, medicine, and hygiene supplies are costly and sometimes difficult to obtain. The financial assistance delivered by the Lenny Peters Foundation is often the only outside help these individuals receive. Others get some state or national funding, but only enough to survive.

In South Africa, Director Susan Jacob leads the Lenny Peters Foundation Homes. Operating after-school programs that offer a safe place for school-age children from some of the poorest communities on the outskirts of Johannesburg, the Homes represent for some children their only meal of the day and the only tutoring they will receive outside of their classrooms.

Jacob describes the services the South Africa Team is able to provide as a "true grace and blessing to be able to be part of the growth of these impoverished children, (many) who come from broken homes."

That blessing extends to single parents and, in some cases, close relatives raising the children, who struggle to care for them on their own despite their best efforts and intentions. Beyond the tangibles provided by the Foundation and its team members, perhaps the most significant gift the children receive is the knowledge that they are loved and genuinely cared for.

For many of us whose basic needs are and have always been met, so much is taken for granted: shelter, warmth, and access to water and food, clean clothes, education, and health care.

For those who have never known these comforts or who cling with desperation to the few they can obtain, the service and support received from the Lenny Peters Foundation and its gracious team members are a lifeline sent from God, by way of—although he would never call himself one —another angel without wings.

**100% of the proceeds from the sale of this book
go to support orphan children and cancer patients**

Scan the QR code below to visit the
Lenny Peters Foundation website
and learn more about who we serve and how.

LennyPetersFoundation.org